## Sappho's Immortal Daughters

Greetings wherever you are, lady, greetings as to a god:
for your songs, your immortal daughters, are with us still.

—*Dioscorides (3rd century BCE)*

# SAPPHO'S
## *Immortal Daughters*

Margaret Williamson

HARVARD UNIVERSITY PRESS
*Cambridge, Massachusetts · London, England*
1995

Ezra Pound's "Papyrus" is reprinted by permission of New
Directions Publishing Group and Faber and Faber Ltd.
Josephine Balmer's translations of Sappho are reprinted
by permission of Bloodaxe Books Ltd.

Library of Congress Cataloging-in-Publication Data

Williamson, Margaret
Sappho's immortal daughters / Margaret Williamson.
    p.  cm.
Includes bibliographical references and index.
ISBN 0-674-78912-1 (alk. paper)
1. Sappho—Criticism and interpretation.  2. Love poetry, Greek—
Women authors—History and criticism.  3. Songs, Greek—Women
authors—History and criticism.  4. Women—Greece—Sexual behavior—
History.  5. Women and literature—Greece—History.  6. Sappho—
Contemporary Greece.  7. Sappho—Criticism, textual.  8. Sappho—In
literature.  9. Sex in literature.  10. Sappho—In art.  I. Title.
        PA409.W55  1995
        884'.01—dc20
        95-20124

*For my mother*

1910–1995

# Contents

# Preface

SAPPHO'S WORK, LIKE that of most of her contemporaries, survives only in fragments. It has always seemed to me paradoxical that the poetry of this period should be the province of one of the most blithely confident branches of classical scholarship. Faced with these collections of tattered fragments, scholars have continually laid optimistic claim to the truth each time they manage to sketch in a missing letter or piece together a new hypothesis. In today's critical climate, such claims become ever harder to maintain, and this is perhaps especially true for a feminist, who should know if anyone does that all readers have motives. So my own attempt to fill in the gaps about Sappho demands some comment.

I set out hoping to deal with her reputation in later European literature as well as in antiquity. I ran out of time and will (like Sappho's first editor, Henri Estienne) have to leave that to others. In pursuit of that aim, though, I sat one day in the British Library reading what might be regarded as the first modern commentary on Sappho: a treatise written in Latin in 1485 by G. Merula (which turned out to be mainly on Ovid). I had been alerted to its existence by a book written in the late nineteenth century by a Hampstead doctor and Sappho enthusiast, Henry Wharton. Since Wharton also read Merula in the British Library, and since the library possesses only two copies, there was a good chance that I, a century later, was handling the same copy of the book.

The link thus formed between me and my two predecessors gave me a vivid sense of our interdependence: as if by, as it were, linking hands we could form a chain that reached back into the past and might ultimately even touch Sappho's era. At the same time, it struck me how much a product of our own circumstances each of us was: the early humanist with his competitive polemics against other scholars; the Victorian amateur with a classical education, and enough leisure from his profession to become an expert on Sappho; and me, a feminist academic writing in the late twentieth century. And each of us was engaging Sappho in a dialogue that reflected the preoccupations of our own lives no less than hers.

The chain will continue: other generations will recreate Sappho in their own image. But in the meantime, and for the moment, I offer this one, written with as much attention to scholarship and care for accuracy as I could manage, but also with a sense of the continuing power and significance of her image. Without the social and political changes of the last half century, it would have been much harder for a woman who, like me, did not come from an established upper- or middle-class background to write this (or any) book. So I have had my own stake in straining to recover that earlier woman's voice and to understand what enabled it—a task made all the more rewarding by the fact that she really is (they were right about that) an extraordinary poet. I have been mindful too of the pioneer status that Sappho has for lesbian women. A remark made in a lecture by Judith Butler stayed with me: à propos of her teenage self-recognition as lesbian she said, "As far as I knew there was only me and a woman called Sappho—but she apparently died a few centuries back."

I take full responsibility for this book, but I am glad to acknowledge at least some of the others who have helped to write it. I could not have written Chapter 2, on the history of Sappho's texts, without the expert and unfailing guidance of Dominic Montserrat, who provided a wealth of information on all matters papyrological and commented on the whole book in draft.

I am especially grateful to Sue Blundell, who not only read drafts but allowed me to read in manuscript parts of her own recently published book on Greek women. The following have provided numerous references, given or lent books, read drafts, and corrected mistakes: Eileen Cadman, Ettore Cingano, Philip DeSouza, Felicity Edholm, Lucy Goodison, Maurice Howard, Stephen Instone, Mandy Merck, David Norbrook, Gill Spraggs, Oliver Taplin. Professor Keith deVries at the University of Pennsylvania kindly answered questions about vase paintings. Special thanks to Ruth Petrie and Robin Osborne, whose comments greatly improved the manuscript in an earlier incarnation, and to Helene Foley and Mary Lefkowitz for more recent advice. And thanks to all the other friends and colleagues, too many to mention here, who encouraged me by always taking an interest.

I have some debts to institutions too. St. Mary's University College gave me as much relief as was possible in these straitened times, and I am grateful to all my colleagues for their support. The British School at Athens provided much practical assistance, and the librarians at the Institute of Classical Studies went out of their way to help, as they always do.

I hope you will find our work worthwhile.

# Note on Sappho's Texts

The texts of Sappho's poems, especially those that survive on papyrus, are all damaged, and they are printed in Greek with a multitude of editorial markings to show gaps and reconstructions. I illustrate some of these marks in Chapter 2 (the Hamlet papyrus); they are explained in the Reading Notes.

Where I quote Sappho's poems for the purpose of detailed discussion (in Chapters 2 and 5), I use a simplified set of these editorial conventions as a guide to the state of the original text. It is not always possible to match exactly their position in the Greek, but they are designed to give some sense of what it is like to read these poems in the original. In deciding where to add them I have used the Greek text printed in David Campbell's Loeb Library edition.

| | |
|---|---|
| [ ] | Material inside brackets added by editor or translator |
| . . . | Gap in text of one line or less |
| ( ) | Lines missing or badly damaged |

Occasionally I add in italics words or phrases that exist in the Greek text but were omitted in the translation quoted.

All titles given for Sappho's poems are modern additions.

# Introduction

THE GREEK POET SAPPHO lived on the island of Lesbos around the turn of the seventh and sixth centuries BCE. She composed lyric poetry (that is, songs with lyre accompaniment) which was collected into nine books by scholars in Alexandria a few centuries later, and she was the most highly regarded woman poet of Greek and Roman antiquity. Only a fraction of her output has survived, and almost all of what now exists is in fragments.

On this bare statement most scholars would be able to agree. But it is impossible to go much beyond it without venturing into controversy. Take the biographical information available about Sappho. Antiquity's accumulated wisdom on the subject appears in a Byzantine encyclopedia, the *Suda*, which was compiled in the tenth century CE from earlier sources. The entry on Sappho reads:

Daughter of Simon or, according to others, of Eumenus or Eerigyius or Ecrytus or Semus or Camon or Etarchus or Scamandronymus; her mother was Cleis; native of Lesbos, from the city of Eresus. Lyric poetess, active in the 42nd Olympiad [612–608 BCE], when Alcaeus, Stesichorus and Pittacus also lived. She had three brothers, Larichus, Charaxus and Eurygius. She was married to a very wealthy man called Cercylas, who traded from Andros, and had a daughter by him who was called Cleis. She had three companions and friends, Atthis, Telesippa and Megara, and acquired a bad reputation for her shameful friendship with them. Her pupils were Anagora from Miletus, Gongyla from Colophon, Euneica from Salamis. She wrote nine books of lyric poetry. She invented the plectrum. She also wrote epigrams, elegiacs, iambics and solo songs.

(test. 2)

Together with an earlier text of similar length, dating from seven or so centuries earlier (test. 1), this is one of the main sources of information about Sappho's life. Despite its authoritative tone, however, most of its details are open to some kind of doubt. The list of possibilities for her father's name, first of all, is an open admission of ignorance. There are few other sources on her mother's name, though nothing to contradict this version either. Then come her brothers, perhaps the best attested of her relatives; other sources agree on their names, and at least one brother is mentioned in the surviving poems. Sappho's daughter Cleis appears at first to be a similar case, with her name mentioned twice in the poet's own words. But even this evidence is fallible. Apart from the tricky question of how far poetry can be read as autobiography, the word used of Cleis in the poems is *pais* (child), which might have been used of a young girl by her older lover. It is not impossible that some earlier commentator, constructing biography from poetry as so many did, misunderstood the word and so put into circulation the idea that Sappho had a daughter called Cleis. Finally, her supposed husband, never mentioned in her poetry, has a name that looks decidedly suspicious. "Cercylas from the island of Andros," translatable as "Prick from the Isle of Man," may simply be an obscene pun dreamed up by one of the Athenian comic playwrights who, two hundred or so years after her death, made Sappho the subject of some of their bawdy and outrageous inventions.

The list of dubious points in the *Suda* entry continues. A few other sources give Sappho's birthplace as Mytilene, not Eresus.

On the nine books of poetry there is independent evidence, but Sappho did not assemble them herself. The story about the invention of the plectrum (an implement for plucking stringed instruments) may be based on confusion with a similar word for a type of lyre. Finally, the statements about her "shameful friendship" with her companions are made from such a hostile viewpoint that their meaning is far from clear, especially since the word used for companion could also, in the Greek of a later period, mean courtesan.

I shall not be tackling all of these conundrums. My focus is not on Sappho's life but on her poetry and the culture that produced it, so that many of them can be left to one side. The target of the book is in a sense its last chapter, in which I take a selection of Sappho's poems and explore their significance in their own cultural context; the earlier chapters prepare the ground. Chapter 3 is a general account of the social and political background, including the all-important question of how a woman might have access to the public medium of song; in Chapter 4 I turn to some perennially controversial questions about the sexual content of her poetry. The biographical tradition is tangential to much of this discussion.

And yet the more general problems raised by the *Suda* entry cannot be ignored. As even these few details show, every shred of information about Sappho has already passed through countless hands, all of which have left their mark. This applies to the very words she composed. The texts of her poems have not been miraculously revealed to us in a state of pristine wholeness, as the merest glance at a page of their fragmentary remains shows. But the gaps in the texts reveal only one aspect of their history. Another is discussed in Chapter 2, which outlines the routes by which Sappho's surviving work has reached the twentieth century and the ways in which it has been shaped along the way by scholars, excavators, editors, and interpreters.

Their judgments share an important feature with the *Suda* entry: they are often influenced by quite another strand of thinking about Sappho. Alongside the poet, other legendary Sapphos emerge through history. Sappho the tragic lover and Sappho the epitome of sexual scandal have had an imaginative life often quite independent of her poetry, flourishing even in periods when there was almost no knowledge of it. Created out of the aspirations, fears, preconceptions, and fantasies of their times, they have also had a profound impact on the way in which her poems were understood and transmitted. I begin, then, with the fictions about Sappho that arose in antiquity, whose influence on the understanding of her work can be detected right up to our own time.

# 1. The Legend

ONE OF THE best-known modern images for Sappho was created by Monique Wittig and Sande Zveig in their *Lesbian Peoples: Materials for a Dictionary* (1980). While the female figures mentioned in her surviving fragments—Andromeda, Gongyla, Gorgo—receive separate entries quoting her words about them, Sappho's own name heads a blank page, a witty reminder to the reader that most of her poetry has been lost. There is a second way too in which it can be taken: as an emblem of the difficulties besetting any attempt to approach the historical figure of this illustrious woman writer. Some of the difficulties do indeed arise from blanks, from the absence of reliable information about many aspects of her life and cultural milieu. But the image can also mislead. Over the two and a half millennia separating Sappho's time from ours, generations of readers and writers have been far from content to leave that page empty. On the contrary, Sappho is a figure who has attracted a wondrous variety of fictions, and who has been revered or condemned with equal passion, and many of these fictions and fantasies are woven into traditions about her life and interpretations of her work. Anyone who wants to engage with the realities of Sappho's life and work, then, must first engage with the fictions. As we follow the twists and turns of her fortunes, the question must often arise: whose image has most often been inscribed on the blank page, hers or that of her readers?

## Sappho in Vase Paintings

Early images of Sappho, in the most literal sense, begin with representations on Athenian vases. On the first such vase to survive, from the end of the sixth century BCE, she is shown holding a lyre in one hand (fig. 1). This is a standard way of representing anyone concerned with poetry: the mythical poet Orpheus, the Muses, and the god Apollo are among those usually shown in this way. In her other hand she holds a plectrum with which to pluck the strings, and above it is written her name.

The portrait is not especially prepossessing, and it might be tempting to think that the artist has tried to represent the real Sappho's appearance: many centuries later she was described, by the poet Ovid among others, as dark, short, and ugly (Ovid, *Heroides* 15.31–35; test. 1). But such accounts were recorded many centuries after her death, and this early portrait closely resembles other images of the period, in which there was no tradition of realistic portraiture. Above all, even this relatively early image was created almost a century after Sappho wrote. The vase is more important as evidence that her fame as a poet was taking root in Athens, a city whose status as a major cultural center over the next few centuries became crucial in preserving her reputation and works.

A second vase, produced in the early fifth century, shows her once again holding lyre and plectrum, and again labeled (fig. 2). This time she is represented in a more obviously idealized way, and there is an important addition: the figure of a male poet with whom Sappho seems to be conversing. His label identifies him as the poet Alcaeus, who lived and wrote on Lesbos when Sappho did. There is little on the vase itself to show what relationship is imagined between the two poets. In reality they are not likely to have performed together, since they composed mainly for audiences of their own sex. But the portrayal suggests a personal dialogue, and as such it marks a crucial move in the fictionalizing of Sappho. From now on, her biography and—

since she writes so much about love—her love life begins to arouse at least as much interest as her poetry. But, at the beginning, her lovers were all men.

In the fourth and third centuries, not only Alcaeus but several other male poets were said to have been in love with Sappho. In some cases we even have snatches of dialogue or poetry supposedly addressed by the lovers to each other. Alcaeus, for example, is said to have addressed her as "violet-haired, holy, sweetly-smiling Sappho" (384). Unfortunately for the plausibility of most of these stories, Alcaeus is the only one of her so-called lovers who actually coincided with her in time and place. Anacreon, said to have been a rival for her love, lived in the late sixth century; two others, the satiric writers Archilochus and Hipponax, lived earlier and later, respectively, than Sappho; and all but Alcaeus came from different parts of the Greek world.

A certain amount of vagueness about dates can be attributed to the legendary status that Sappho had already acquired: she is not the only celebrity of the period around whom a host of anecdotes, often apocryphal, grew up. But we are probably also dealing with unabashed fiction. Stories about Sappho's romantic liaisons with poets seem to have begun in earnest in the fourth century, when she became a popular subject of comedies in Athens; we know of at least six plays named after her, though little of their contents survives. Over the century Athenian comedy gradually changed from a high-spirited mixture of bawdiness, topical satire, no-holds-barred caricature, and mythical extravagance to a much more restrained comedy of manners. Such fragments as remain of comedies about Sappho suggest, however, that there is a good deal of the old comic spirit in them: one fragment, for example, deals with a boy prostitute who pays in trade for his dinner (Ephippus, *Sappho*). Like any other prominent figure, gods and heroes included, Sappho was probably fair game for these playwrights' flights of caricature and fantasy. The fantasy is particularly evident in her association with yet another male lover, the ferryman Phaon of myth.

## Sappho and Phaon

The story of Sappho and Phaon turned out to be one of the most durable fictions about her, and it almost certainly arose in the fourth century. Phaon's story, which is known only from much later sources, goes as follows. A ferryman on the island of Lesbos, he is approached by the goddess Aphrodite in the guise of an old woman. He ferries her across the water without asking for payment, and in return she transforms him into a beautiful youth with whom all the women of Lesbos fall in love. Some versions of the story indicate that Aphrodite herself is in love with him, so that Phaon's story follows a pattern also found in the myths of Adonis, Tithonus, and Endymion, all young mortals loved by goddesses.

The myths surrounding these young men evidently had a good deal of currency in the fourth century. There was, to begin with, the festival of the Adonia: women gathered to mourn the death of Aphrodite's beloved Adonis, in what were evidently rowdy all-night celebrations. And there were quite a number of comedies touching on these youths. We know of one *Endymion,* two entitled *Adonis,* and at least two about Phaon. At some point Sappho and Phaon, who may have entered the comic repertoire separately, were linked. Sappho became identified as one of the women in love with Phaon, and by conflation with another strand of mythical tradition, she was said to have thrown herself off the cliff at Leucas after being spurned. Three comedies of which little now exists but the title, *The Woman of Leucas,* probably refer to this episode, and the first surviving account is by the comic playwright Menander, who refers to Leucas as the place

> where they say Sappho,
> hunting proud Phaon,
> first flung herself, goaded by desire,
> from the bright cliff.
>    (test. 23)

The link between Sappho and Phaon probably arose from her poetry. We are told that she referred to several young men who were beloved of goddesses; and although no surviving poem mentions Phaon, one ancient commentator tells us that she often "composed songs about her love for him" (211a). But this statement almost certainly depends on a misreading of her poetry as autobiography, and the Leucadian leap undoubtedly belongs to the realm of outright legend. What is interesting is the significance attached to her romance with Phaon in fourth-century Athens and later. What was it that gave this, out of all the liaisons foisted upon Sappho, such a hold on the imagination?

Perhaps part of the answer lies in the richly suggestive image of the leap from the cliff: Sappho's suicidal plunge has been used to signify all manner of things, from guilty despair to passionate abandon to poetic inspiration. But another clue can be found in the differences between Phaon and Sappho's other supposed lovers, which go beyond the fact that he is the only purely mythical figure. In the late fifth and early fourth centuries BCE, before his appearances in comedy and before we hear of his link with Sappho, Phaon is represented on a series of Athenian vases. On one he is shown in his boat, waiting to take Aphrodite aboard; on others he is surrounded by adoring women and sometimes by symbolic figures such as the Erotes, personifications of love.

Phaon in these scenes cuts a very different figure from Alcaeus on the vase mentioned earlier. He is a curiously feminine figure, slightly plump and in a passive pose. His body is often turned almost full front toward the viewer, a position usually adopted by female figures. Above all, he is unlike most adult males on vases (except when shown getting married) in being beardless. This both makes him, like the ideal bridegroom, an erotically appealing figure and suggests that he has not yet attained adult status. The significance of this second aspect is brought out by the inscription appearing above his head on one vase (fig. 3): *Phaōn kalos* (Phaon is beautiful). This formula—the ancient equivalent of an initialed heart pierced by an arrow—is common on vases, and it often identifies a boy as the object of an older man's desire, perhaps in this case the owner of the vase.

According to ancient codes of sexual etiquette (though not necessarily practice), the roles of the two participants in an erotic relationship are quite distinct. Where two males are concerned, they are generally of different ages and status: a youth, the beloved *(erōmenos)*, whose role is only to be desired, and an older man, the lover *(erastēs)*, who actively pursues him. In heterosexual liaisons, it is normal for the woman to be the beloved and the man the lover. What is distinctive about Phaon on this vase is that he is shown as the beloved, an object of desire both inside and outside the frame of the picture. Within it, the part of lover is played both by the lustful goat-god Pan, who gazes down on Phaon from the top left, and also by a woman, who tries to embrace him.

There is a clear contrast, then, between Phaon's sexual status and that of Sappho's other lovers, marked both visually and verbally. Alcaeus is a bearded mature man; Phaon is beardless. Archilochus and Hipponax are described as Sappho's lovers, *erastai* (test. 8); Phaon is an object of desire for others both male and female. But whereas a passive role is acceptable for a young man on the verge of adulthood, the corresponding active role is not generally thought appropriate for a woman. This means that Sappho in pursuit of Phaon is breaching the social codes governing gender roles.

This is not to say that there were no channels for exploring, in fantasy and sometimes in real life, variants on these social roles: these are the dominant images of sexual relations, but not necessarily the only ones. The vase itself shows that there were, at least in imagination, other possibilities, and so does the Adonia, which several sources describe with more than a hint of disapproval. Another specialized context in which fantasy could, in carnival fashion, be let loose was comedy itself, performed for a predominantly male or possibly even male-only audience, which turns the official rules upside down. Women were supposed in everyday life to show modesty and self-restraint; comedy presents a mirror image of this male-centered ideology, with its stock in trade of unruly, tipsy, and randy women. A scene from one of the *Phaon* plays illustrates this. Aphrodite comes out of her shrine and addresses a crowd of Phaon's fans who are all apparently the worse for drink. If they want to get their hands on Phaon, she says, they will have to make the appropriate gifts to herself and to other gods. Her list, a parody of real offerings to gods, becomes more crude and outrageous as it goes on, and she ends by instructing the women to make payments to some very unusual deities:

> One drachma to Bendoverbackwards
> and three obols to Arseintheair;
> and for Rideacockhorse, incense and a skin (a foreskin,
>      that is).
> That's the damage: once you've paid you can come in,
> Otherwise, I'm afraid you'll just have to fuck . . . . . off.
>      (Plato, *Phaon*)

In actively pursuing Phaon, the playwrights' Sappho is in one sense just conforming to this comic stereotype. But this is not the only context in which she takes a more assertive role in love than was thought appropriate for a woman. Later I will consider the range of erotic roles in her poetry and the ways in which it may have helped to generate the comic image of her. But in following her fortunes into Roman culture, we shall find that she continues to be a figure who breaches prescribed gender roles. Outside the context of comic license, this transgression is not always viewed so benignly—but it is probably a major reason for the fascination she continues to arouse.

Even as these biographical fantasies were multiplying, a parallel strand of interest in Sappho was content to commemorate her as a great poet. The philosopher Plato, in the fourth century, though he like everyone else associates her with love, treats her as an authority on the subject, not just a practitioner. In his dialogue the *Phaedrus,* she is mentioned as one of the "wise men and women of old" (235bc) whose views might be consulted on the matter. And she continued to be honored both in her native Lesbos and elsewhere: the eminent Athenian sculptor Silanion, for example, made a statue of her (test. 24). But it was in the Hellenistic period that her reputation as a poet really flowered. It was also then, as far as we can tell, that she began to be a model and point of comparison for other women writers.

## Sappho in Hellenistic Poetry

As Alexander the Great's conquests were bringing the Greek world together into one empire, Greek culture was entering a new phase. In the last two centuries BCE, Athens was no longer the undisputed cultural center of the Greek world. It was rivaled and eventually overtaken in importance by other cities, notably the one founded in northern Egypt by Alexander and named after him.

Alexandria became home to a literary culture more dependent on the written word than any before it: more bookish and far more conscious of inheriting a cherished literary tradition that went back to Homer and before. One symptom of this was the great zeal shown by the scholars of the time in compiling editions of the great poets of the past, including Sappho. Hand in hand with this activity went a new attitude to poetry, which became the province of a learned few. The scholar-poets from Alexandria and other cities wrote for a small audience of cognoscenti who would appreciate their sophistication in imitating and alluding to earlier literature.

Because of their close links with literary scholarship, one might expect Hellenistic attitudes to Sappho to arise more directly from her own poetry than that of the Athenian comic playwrights, and to a certain extent this is true. It is at this point, for example, that other poets, such as Theocritus, start to include learned imitations of Sappho in their own works. Others write poems addressed to or about her which are largely free of biographical fantasies, and even of references to her life. Instead they are concerned with another kind of myth: Sappho as a poet of legendary, indeed divine, powers. Their rendering of this myth reflects both on the glory of the tradition in which they write and—they hope—on the skill with which they themselves develop it.

A genre whose popularity burgeoned at this time was the epigram, a type of short poem often used for commemorative purposes, such as dedications of monuments or inscriptions on tombstones, though the occasion might also be a fictional one. Among the hundreds of surviving poems of this kind, there are many written about famous figures of the past. It is a measure of the canonical status now acquired by Sappho that, as well as having some elegiac epigrams passed off under her name, she was addressed in several of these celebratory poems.

One of the earliest in existence, written in the late third century BCE, is an elaborate and ingenious compliment:

> O Sappho, sweetest support for young passions,
> you must surely be keeping company with the Muses,
> honoured by ivied Helicon and by Pieria,
> for the songs of the Muse from Eresus equal theirs;
> or else it's the god of weddings, Hymen,
> who stands by you over the bridal bed, torch in hand;
> or else you share Aphrodite's weeping for young Adonis,
> and so come to see the holy grove of the blessed.
> Greetings wherever you are, lady, greetings as to a god:
> for your songs, your immortal daughters, are with us still.
> (Dioscorides, *Greek Anthology* 7.407; test. 58)

The suggestion that poetry defies death by outliving its author was a commonplace in many earlier poets, Sappho included. Common too was the belief that poetic skill was bestowed by the gods, especially the nine Muses. But it is typical of Hellenistic poetry to turn these traditional ideas into poetic conceits and give them a new twist. The divine assistance that Sappho receives is presented conventionally enough to begin with: like many

*The Legend*

before her, she consorts with the Muses on the mountains they frequent, Helicon and Pieria. But then this idea, once presented, is capped: Sappho is so great a poet that she must be a Muse herself, and later in the poem it is she who assists a god, Aphrodite, in mourning Adonis' death, not the other way around. The whole poem thus becomes a monument not only to Sappho but also to its author's learning and wit.

Dioscorides' celebratory poem is one of the earliest to survive and is also more closely linked to Sappho's own work than most others. It refers not only to her love poetry (in the first line Sappho's verse seems to be thought of as soothing, by giving voice to, the torments of young lovers) but to two other kinds of poem of which examples by Sappho still exist: wedding songs and laments for Adonis. But later poems of this type, which continued to be written well into the Christian era, are less closely based on her work: they simply recast the same set of overblown compliments. Sappho's fame and works are (like those of many other poets) immortal; she is comparable with Homer; she is the only woman among the nine great lyric poets of archaic Greece. Above all, the idea that she is a tenth Muse (as others were called the fourth Grace or a second Helen) quickly became a cliché. A rather tame version of this is attributed to Plato, but was probably the work of a Hellenistic author:

> Some say there are nine Muses; but how careless!
> See: Sappho of Lesbos is the tenth.
> (test. 60)

The version by Antipater of Sidon in the second century is a little more inventive, encapsulated in a neat two-liner:

> Hearing the songs of honey-voiced Sappho, the goddess
>     Memory stood amazed.
> [Mother of nine immortal Muses], she wondered: could
>     there, on earth, be a tenth?
> (*Greek Anthology* 9.66)

Commonplace though they became, these images raise some important questions about perceptions of women as authors. The grand gesture of describing Sappho as the tenth Muse is perhaps double-edged. As well as paying her an extravagant compliment, it may also indicate a difficulty in thinking of real women as poets: in order to write as she did, Sappho has passed beyond the bounds of ordinary humanity. The image also, of course, presents her as a unique figure, and one without successors.

But Dioscorides' epigram contains a second and rather different image of female creativity: Sappho's poems are her "daughters." A similar idea is found, intriguingly, in a passage attributed to the character Sappho in a fourth-century comedy. The poet puts to her companions a riddle:

A female creature there is, who keeps her infants
beneath her robes. They are voiceless, and yet
their cry resounds over land and sea;
they speak to whomever they will, and even those
who are absent or deaf are able to hear them.
    (Antiphanes, *Sappho*)

In the play Sappho's father offers a solution from public, and therefore exclusively masculine, life: he guesses that the creature is the city (*polis*, whose gender in Greek is feminine) and her children its public speakers. Sappho scornfully dismisses this answer and gives the right one. The female creature is a letter (*epistolē*, also feminine), and the offspring she carries around, or puts into circulation, are written characters. Though voiceless, they can speak to those far away, and their recipients can read them without a bystander hearing—that is, in silence.

As an image of dissemination through writing, this could rival the better-known version of Plato in the *Phaedrus*, written at about the same time. In Plato's version, the written letters are the orphaned sons of an absent father, without whose guidance they go around the world speaking indiscriminately to all and sundry (275de). In *Sappho* they have an ambiguous relationship

*The Legend*

with their "mother," whose babies can be thought of as nestled either in her garments or in her womb (the words used suggest both). The fact that Sappho's riddle appears in a popular entertainment suggests that these metaphorical attempts to grapple with the profound effects of the use of writing were widespread. Perhaps, as so often, it is the biases of the process of transmission which have privileged Plato's masculinist version rather than more popular, and female, versions such as that attributed here to Sappho.

This image too points to a conceptual difficulty both for and about female writers. Sappho's riddle draws from biology an image for a cultural process; but on the cultural level, in a patrilineal and patriarchal society, motherhood is a problematic image for inheritance. In Greek social life, almost all women's daughters were destined when they married to pass from the guardianship of their father to that of their husband, leaving their mother's household probably for good; the children they bore would be the vehicle of men's inheritance, not their own.

Yet the riddle also suggests the means by which a tradition of women's writing could be created and maintained. Women poets were said to have existed in Greece from very early times, though little or no work has survived. But it is only in the Hellenistic period that the idea arises of a specifically female poetic inheritance. The poet thought of as founding it is, of course, Sappho, and the medium of its transmission is writing.

## Sappho and Hellenistic Women Writers

The question of how and what women could compose is partly a question about their access to public discourse. But for the Hellenistic period, there is little doubt that the evolution of poetic composition into a primarily written art made it easier for women to participate, and facilitated the sense of a female cultural inheritance. The poetic genres of earlier periods—epic and tragedy, for example—often involved performance, publicly sponsored, before a large audience. The detachment of a form such as the epigram from these grand public occasions meant that it could be put to all kinds of different uses, including private and a new range of fictional ones. Writing also made possible a sense of dialogue through time, as illustrated in Dioscorides' epigram.

Poets and their works tended, like the Muses, to come in nines. By the end of the Hellenistic period, there were nine canonical writers of archaic lyric as well as nine officially great female poets. The women's names are given in an epigram by Antipater of Thessalonica, who wrote around the time of the birth of Christ:

> These are women of heavenly voice, reared on songs
> by Helicon and by Pieria, Macedon's crag:
> Praxilla, Moero, Anyte's lips, the female Homer;
> Sappho, the glory of Lesbos's women with beautiful hair;
> Erinna, renowned Telesilla, and you, Corinna,
> who sang of Athena's shield of furious war.
> Nossis of feminine tongue, and Myrtis who sang so sweetly:
> all of them crafted pages that live forever.
> Nine were the Muses whom Heaven brought forth: nine too
> are these, borne by Earth for mortals' undying delight.
> (Greek Anthology 9.26)

Of these, about half (there is some uncertainty over dates) are Hellenistic; the rest, including Sappho, are earlier.

The four poets who can be fairly confidently described as Hellenistic are Moero, Anyte, Erinna, and Nossis. All four lived and wrote outside the main urban and literary centers, and all but Erinna wrote epigrams: Erinna was known mainly for a long poem written in hexameters (the meter of Homer), lamenting her childhood friend Baucis, who died soon after marriage. It is Erinna and Nossis who are most explicitly linked with Sappho.

Erinna, like Sappho, was the subject of celebratory epigrams by male authors, in which many of the same motifs recur. Her poems too are immortal; she dances with the Pierian Muses; her hexameters equal Homer's; she distills drops of honey (a traditional metaphor) in her writing. So it is all the more striking that

*The Legend*

she is not apostrophized as a Muse: instead Sappho herself, the original tenth Muse, is the point of comparison. An anonymous poem introduces Erinna's work as a "Lesbian honeycomb," and since she herself almost certainly came from another island, this is undoubtedly an allusion to Sappho. It is developed further in the poem's final couplet:

> As far as Sappho outdoes Erinna in lyrics,
> Thus far is Erinna superior in hexameters.
> (test. 35)

No doubt misled by this association, Byzantine writers called her Sappho's contemporary, and both she and Anyte were said to come from the city of Mytilene on Lesbos.

But it is Nossis, writing in Locri in southern Italy, whose links with Sappho are the most interesting, not least because they are made by the poet herself. Nossis' name was accompanied, in Antipater's epigram, by an adjective meaning something like "of womanly speech"; and Meleager, who put together an anthology of epigrams around 100 BCE, says in introducing her poems that "Eros himself melted the wax" for the tablets on which she wrote (*Greek Anthology* 4.1.10). Both associations—with women and with love—are borne out in her epigrams. Most of them are clearly woman-oriented, dealing with subjects such as portrait statues of women and dedications and prayers to Hera, Artemis, and particularly Aphrodite.

In one of her dedicatory poems, Nossis herself addresses the question of a female poetic inheritance using the metaphor of maternity. The poem, addressing Hera, asks her to accept a robe woven by Nossis and her mother:

> Most honoured Hera, you who often descend from heaven
>   to survey your Lacinian shrine fragrant with incense,
> receive this linen robe which, with her noble daughter
>   Nossis, Theophilis daughter of Cleocha wove for you.
> (*Greek Anthology* 6.265)

*Sappho's Immortal Daughters*

Weaving is often used as an image both for women's cultural achievement and for poetic composition. Homer evokes both meanings at once when in book 3 of the *Iliad* he describes Helen weaving in a tapestry the story—her story—of the Trojan war. In placing such emphasis on female descent in the context of a poem about weaving, the poem hints also at the transmission of the craft of poetry from grandmother and mother to daughter.

This makes it all the more significant that Nossis elsewhere claims poetic affiliation with Sappho. In the poem that probably prefaced her collection, she both claims love as her subject matter and evokes Sappho by association:

> Nothing is sweeter than love. All other delights come second:
>   even honey I spit from my mouth.
> This Nossis says: whomever Aphrodite has not loved
>   knows not her flowers and what roses they are.
> (*Greek Anthology* 5.170)

The interpretation of the last two lines is made problematic by a garbled text. It seems likely, though, that the roses are Nossis' own erotic poems, which can only be appreciated by someone (of unspecified gender) who has experienced the favors of Aphrodite. Roses, as well as having erotic connotations, also evoke Sappho, whose poems are referred to as roses both by herself and by Meleager in the preface to his anthology.

Sappho is linked with flower imagery in another poem in which Nossis explicitly creates a connection with her predecessor. Here she uses the common literary device of mimicking a funerary inscription addressed to a passerby:

> If, stranger, you sail to Mytilene of the lovely dances
>   to seek inspiration from the flower of Sappho's graces,
> say there that Locri has borne one dear to the Muses and to
>     her;
>   know that my name is Nossis, and then go.
> (*Greek Anthology* 7.718)

*The Legend*

Again some details of the text are uncertain, but it is clear that Nossis is claiming a bond with Sappho through her poetry. Yet this bond is one of which Sappho, within the fiction of the poem, is not yet aware; news of it is entrusted, after Nossis' death, to the whim of a passing (male) stranger, who may or may not travel as far as Mytilene. There could hardly be a more poignant image for, on one hand, Sappho's importance to later women writers and, on the other, the fragility of the tradition she inaugurates, which is in the hands of men. The fate of Sappho's literary daughters is uncertain indeed.

Of the writers so far discussed, Nossis is the one who alludes most closely to Sappho's writings, so that to some extent she belongs with literary imitators of Sappho rather than with the fiction makers. I have included her, though, because of her importance in the history of Sapphic images, and there is another respect in which she can shed light on their history. Nossis' claim to be the author of love poetry is hardly backed up by her surviving epigrams, so it is likely that her erotic poetry has been lost. In view of her declared affinity with Sappho, it has been suggested that this poetry was, like Sappho's, lyric and, more important, that it was addressed to women. If this is so, it would help to explain the manner in which Nossis herself, together with Erinna, is mentioned in the work of a writer from nearby Sicily who was probably a near-contemporary.

Herodas was the author of a series of mimes, short dramatic dialogues whose content is humorous and often sexually titillating. One has a pimp demanding payment from a sea captain who has assaulted one of his girls; in another a woman berates her slave for his sexual infidelities to her. Mimes 6 and 7 are about a cobbler who is also an expert maker of dildoes, and it is here that Nossis and Erinna make an appearance.

In mime 6, a woman called Metro wants to track down the maker of a dildo. It belongs to her friend Coritto, who has hardly had a chance to use it herself before being pressed to lend it out to a series of eager friends. Metro saw it, she says, when "Nossis, daughter of Erinna, had it a couple of days ago" (20–21).

Mime 7 has the shoemaker himself selling to Metro what are eventually revealed to be not shoes but dildoes. In his list of wares appear two items named "nossises" and "baucises" (57–58). There are a few occurrences of both words elsewhere to show that these were indeed types of shoe, perhaps, like Wellingtons, named after an individual. But their appearance together in mime 6 suggests that the two items are double-entendres alluding to Nossis and to Erinna's friend Baucis; and what they have in common is close attachment to female friends.

These allusions, slight as they are, are important as one of the earliest examples of love between women treated as a subject of titillation or scandal. Sappho herself is absent from this scenario except by association: surprising though it may seem, there is no clear evidence that she was explicitly linked with homoeroticism in the Hellenistic or any earlier period. But these allusions make it plausible that she was, and they prefigure the aura of scandal that later came to surround her name, especially in Roman writers. The fact that they are mere asides in the narrative of Metro's and Coritto's desire for an object representing the phallus anticipates another important aspect of the scandal surrounding Sappho. A scene purporting to be about female desire is organized around representations of male sexuality: the two women in mime 6 can hardly wait to get hold of a dildo, and in 7 the names of Nossis and Baucis are made to stand for the phallus. This kind of preoccupation with masculinity continues to pervade accounts of female homoeroticism in later sources as well.

## Sappho in Roman Times

From the first century BCE on, references to Sappho begin to appear in Roman sources, partly because of Greece's massive cultural influence on its conquerors. But Greek culture continued its separate development too, and this is especially evident in references to Sappho.

Among the Greeks, Sappho continued to enjoy a glorious reputation as a poet several centuries into the Roman Empire.

*The Legend*

The geographer Strabo, writing around the beginning of the Christian era, calls her, echoing Hellenistic attitudes, "a marvellous creature" and continues, "in all recorded history I know of no woman who even came close to rivalling her as a poet" (test. 7L). The inhabitants of Mytilene in her native Lesbos used her image on their coinage in the first few centuries CE, and the orator Dio Chrysostom cites her, together with semimythical figures like Semiramis, queen of Babylon, as one of the "illustrious women of old" (64.2). Even when interest in the authors of the past narrowed and those from classical Athens became the most favoured, Sappho remained a canonical figure: the medical writer Galen tells us in the second century CE that you have only to say the Poet and the Poetess, and everyone knows you mean Homer and Sappho (Kühn 4.771).

Sappho also continues, this time mainly in Roman writers, to be mentioned as a model for other women. A humorous glimpse of the aspirations of at least some Roman women can be found in a second-century Greek author, Lucian. He writes satirically about Roman would-be intellectuals who like to establish their cultural credentials by retaining educated Greeks in their entourages. Their claims, though, are bogus, as illustrated by an anecdote about an eminent Greek philosopher who was given no more elevated a task than looking after his mistress' pregnant dog; the wretched man was forced to carry the dog around with him everywhere until, after several days of constantly wetting him, it eventually delivered its puppies in his cloak. Indeed, says Lucian, the women are even worse than the men: all they are after is a reputation for "being cultured, and interested in philosophy, and writing poems not much worse than Sappho's" (On Salaried Posts in Great Houses 36).

Somewhat more serious is the use of Sappho by Roman poets as a model of poetic learning and skill. Catullus in the first century BCE addresses a friend's sweetheart as "more learned than the Sapphic Muse" (test. 56), and a little later Ovid says to a woman poet, possibly his stepdaughter, that if she lives up to her early promise her verse will be inferior only to Sappho's

(*Tristia* 3.7.20). But the comparison soon begins to reflect on more than Sappho's poetic skill. At the end of the first century CE Martial links this with the other strand of her reputation when he says of a contemporary woman writer, Sulpicia:

> with her as fellow-pupil or as teacher, Sappho,
>    you'd be more learned—and you'd be decent too.
>    (*Epigrams* 10.35)

By this time, then, her reputation had, for Romans especially, an unmistakable whiff of sexual scandal to it. It was also firmly in the hands of men: far fewer women authors are heard of in this period, and none of those whose works survive mentions Sappho.

No doubt there are a number of different reasons for the bad reputation that Sappho acquired. One is the preoccupation of the Roman elite with sexual behavior as an index both of individual status and of social and moral order: the back-to-basics laws passed by the emperor Augustus in the late first century concerning marriage and adultery are one illustration. Sappho was on the wrong side of the line in several ways. To begin with, she was Greek; and while, for some Romans, Greek culture was a mark of sophistication, for others it was fundamentally anti-Roman, a source of eastern degeneracy and corruption. Sappho came, too, from an island whose women had long been known not only for their beauty but also for their skill in the arts of (heterosexual) lovemaking.

She was also an educated woman who wrote about love. It is significant that Catullus' pseudonym for the woman to whom many of his love poems are addressed is Lesbia, meaning "the woman from Lesbos." Catullus' Lesbia is presented as a married woman, but one very different from the chaste matrons of early Roman legend; as well as being a connoisseur of poetry, she is also versed in the arts of extramarital amours. While Catullus outraged propriety and social hierarchy by declaring himself her slave in love, others were claiming such relationships—and especially such women—as symbolic of all that was wrong in Roman society. To take Sappho as a standard of female learning was also to associate her with figures like these; and the fact that she was now thought of primarily as a love poet made it all the easier to do so.

But the most important factor was the biographical fictions in which she once again figured. Sappho's image as the lover of Phaon now underwent a renaissance, and she also, concurrently, emerges clearly in the sources as a lover of women. She is shown in both roles in a fictional work of the late first century BCE attributed to the poet Ovid, which became the single most important source of perceptions of Sappho in later times.

## Ovid's Sappho

Ovid's *Heroides* (Letters of the Heroines) is a series of fictional verse epistles from mythical women to their absent lovers. The first is a letter from Penelope to Odysseus; in number 3, which also draws on Homer, the Trojan Briseis writes to Achilles, the Greek hero to whom she was briefly given as war booty; and number 7, based on book 4 of the *Aeneid,* is addressed by Dido to Aeneas. In number 15 the only historical figure in the collection, Sappho, writes to her old comic lover, Phaon. Some think this epistle is not the work of Ovid, but since its authorship makes little practical difference here, I shall treat it as his.

In the scenario of this epistle, Sappho has abandoned her earlier loves, the girls of Lesbos, for Phaon; but he in turn has deserted her and is away in Sicily. In over two hundred lines of elegiac couplets, Sappho pleads with him to return, using a whole range of persuasive techniques. She argues with him, citing her poetic art as an adequate substitute for the beauty she admits she does not possess. She describes her misery and recounts the woes of her life, including Phaon's desertion. She rails against her lot, calls on Venus for help, remembers past bliss, and finally tells of the apparition of a Naiad, who told her to leap from the Leucadian rock as a cure for her love. The epistle closes with a final plea to Phaon to tell her whether she must indeed seek her fate in the waters off Leucas: the reader of course knows that this means her death.

In the account this Sappho gives of herself, there is much to support the image of the dissolute and voluptuous Greek. Sappho is consumed by her passion for Phaon. Without him even her poetic powers are gone, and her daughter, far from being a consolation, is simply another of her burdens. Her misery is demonstrated by the absence of her usual lavish ornament and by her unkempt appearance:

> Around my neck dishevelled ringlets cling
> But on my fingers not a single ring.
> My dress is shabby, no gold ornaments
> Gleam in my hair, and no exotic scents.
> (73–76, tr. Hine)

Worst of all, her lovemaking with Phaon is twice described with a frankness unparalleled anywhere else in the *Heroides,* which was bound to raise eyebrows in Augustan Rome.

But it would be a mistake to take all this at face value. Ovid is the most sophisticated, self-aware, and playful of poets, and like earlier poems in the series this one is full of literary artifice, alluding to earlier poetic traditions. One source is Sappho's own poetry, and even though Ovid had access to far more of it than we do, it is still possible to see that he has worked in a number of allusions to it, from references to the importance of partings and memory in Sappho to imitations of particular passages. But the image they help to create is knowingly and subtly manipulated, as the poem itself declares. Sappho despairingly asks why it is her fate to be so vulnerable to the arrows of love; in reply, Ovid attributes to her what can be read as a commentary on the entire biographical tradition, undercutting it even as he continues it. Perhaps, the poet makes his fictional Sappho say, it is because of the subject matter of her poetry that she is destined

*The Legend*

for passion: she writes of love, and her art has shaped her temperament (83–84).

The other conspicuous piece of ventriloquism in the poem comes at its beginning. The opening lines pose a question to Phaon, as well as to the reader. Did he know who wrote these lines even before reading the name of their author, or did they have to be labeled as—Sappho's? The question of course highlights the fact that the author of Sappho's signature is really Ovid (or perhaps, even better, an imitator of Ovid) and points to another of the games with poetic convention that are going on in this poem.

In the *Amores*, written a decade or so earlier, Ovid took up the persona of the poet-lover found in a series of earlier poets, including Catullus. Like Catullus, he declares himself a slave to his mistress, enraptured when she favors him and in despair when she is faithless. In this poem, too, there are many echoes of the attitudes of an elegiac lover: not only does "Sappho" write in the same meter, but she is subject to the same mercurial shifts of mood, from despair to hope and back again, and capable of deploying the same range of witty hyperbole, ingenious argument, and mythical precedent. She even complains to Phaon that his failure to warn her of his desertion has deprived her of the opportunity to make the usual gestures. All the repertoire of the betrayed poet-lover is there in her list: the tears, the kisses, the tokens, and the injunctions to eternal memory.

In this way Ovid contrives to add yet another twist to the subversion of gender roles that was already implicit in the lover-poet's enslavement to his mistress. As Sappho becomes a slave to her love for Phaon, so he takes on the role of an elegiac mistress. He is not only pretty but adulterous and deceitful too, and Sappho warns the women of Sicily not to believe the kind of blandishments he has falsely lavished on her. But the poet's games with gender and poetic convention reach their height in Sappho herself, whose stance as betrayed lover involves several layers of poetic transvestism. Not only does she confound gender roles by striking some of the poses of male elegiac love poets— but so, by speaking for and through her, does Ovid.

Despite this sleight of hand, the gender roles adopted in the poem are in many ways consistent with those found elsewhere, which takes us back to the reasons for Sappho's scandalous reputation. Within the poem, Sappho incurs disapproval both for her attachment to Phaon and because of her earlier love of her countrywomen. Her brother scorns her passion for Phaon and reproaches her for lamenting him as she might a son who had died, suggesting that it is a matter for shame; later she addresses the women of Lesbos as "you who, in being loved, brought me disgrace" (201).

The image of Sappho mourning over a dead son is only one of many clues to an essential feature of her relationship with Phaon. Ovid repeatedly stresses the disparity of age between them: as in Athenian vase portrayals, Phaon is young, "neither yet a youth nor still a boy" (93); he is only just at puberty, the "age of the first down" on the cheeks and an age that, quite explicitly, arouses desire in mature men, "years such as a man can love" (86). Sappho, by contrast, is a mother, a mature woman, like Aurora and Phoebe, the dawn and moon goddesses (called Eos and Selene by the Greeks) who stole away young men. It is also she, the female partner, who takes the active role: she is the pursuer, whose demand of Phaon is "not to love, but to let yourself be loved" (96). Ovid has, then, taken his cue from Athenian comedy in presenting a Sappho who rejects the sexual passivity appropriate to women.

The poem gives fewer clues as to why her previous love for women is so disgraceful. By this period, however, references to love between women are beginning to appear in other contexts. Some of them suggest that Sappho's love for women is condemned not, as one might have thought, for its differences from her passion for Phaon, but for its similarities.

## Sappho as a Lover of Women

By no means all of the writers who link Sappho with homoeroticism condemn it, as her fictional contemporaries in the *Heroides* do. In Greek authors in particular, we find a range of different attitudes. A fragment of a Greek biography of Sappho, written on papyrus dating from the late second or early third centuries CE, reports some criticism, though apparently it does not share it: "she has been accused by some of being irregular in her ways and a woman-lover" (test. 1). Others, though, treat it in a matter-of-fact way, as shown in a number of comments spread over several centuries after Ovid. Writing in the first to second centuries CE, Plutarch refers to one of her most famous poems as having been occasioned by the appearance of her *erōmenē*, her (female) beloved (*Moralia* 762–763), and a little later Maximus of Tyre compares Socrates' relationship to men with Sappho's to women (test. 20). Two centuries later Themistius, writing a panegyric to a Christian emperor, can still say of Sappho and another poet, Anacreon, that "they are allowed to be immoderate and to exaggerate when praising their darlings *(paidika)*" (*Speeches* 13.170d–171a).

Although these Greek writers show that female homoeroticism did not automatically cause outrage, at the same time they illustrate what helped to arouse it in others. Plutarch and Themistius demonstrate clearly that homoerotic desire is thought of as following the same pattern for women as for men: that is, it is felt by someone senior in age and status for someone younger or socially inferior. This assumption is explicit in Plutarch's use of the term "beloved" in its female form, and Themistius' word "darlings" also usually refers to the same asymmetrical structure.

The implications of this can be seen in a number of other Greek references to homoeroticism from the second century on. One of the fullest is found in Lucian's *Dialogues of the Courtesans,* short prose dialogues similar in form to those of Herodas and drawing much of their material from Greek comedy. In the fifth of these, one professional call girl quizzes another, Leaena, about what happened after a drinking party at which Leaena had been hired to play the lyre by a rich woman from Lesbos called Megilla. There have been rumors that Megilla desires Leaena "like a man," and her friend's suspicions about what that means are strengthened by what she has heard about women from Lesbos: "They say there are in Lesbos women . . . of masculine appearance, who don't want it from men, but sleep with women as if they themselves were men" (*Dialogues of the Courtesans 5*).

Leaena declares herself ashamed to go into detail about her experiences, but she says enough to justify the suspicions. When the party was over, Megilla invited Leaena into bed with her and another woman called Daemonassa. After some energetic foreplay in which both women kissed Leaena "like men," Megilla tore off her wig to reveal a shaved head, asked "Have you ever seen such a fine-looking young man?" and said she was really Megillus, husband of Daemonassa. She then bribed Leaena with presents in order to be allowed to make love to her, responding to Leaena's puzzled questions with an assurance that she was perfectly well equipped to do so: "You'll find I'm just as good as a man: I have something instead of what men have." But Leaena bashfully fails to reveal what this miraculous equipment was.

Although Sappho is not mentioned here, she is again evoked by the reference to women from Lesbos, and this dialogue is the first surviving source to link Lesbos unequivocally with female homoeroticism, rather than general sexual license. (A poem by Anacreon, 358, from the sixth century BCE, may play on this link, but its meaning is disputed: more on this in Chapter 4.) It also makes clear an assumption widely shared by other writers: that a woman who wants to make love to another woman has to play the part of a man. This assumption follows from the fact that the polarities of age and status that are supposed to structure erotic relationships are also gendered: to desire is masculine, to be desired is feminine. Where homosexual liaisons are concerned, this poses an obvious problem, which is circumvented in the case of men by restricting the role of the beloved to those who are too young to be considered men. If two women are erotically involved, however, there is no way out of the presumption that at least one of them is acting as a man.

An episode in Ovid's *Metamorphoses* confirms that what offends in relationships between women is the appropriation of masculine roles. In book 9 he tells the story of Iphis, a Cretan girl whose mother, afraid to tell her husband that she has not given birth to the son he wanted, has passed her daughter off as a boy. Iphis' father betrothes "him" at the age of thirteen to another girl, Ianthe, and the two fall in love. But whereas Ianthe longs for her wedding day, Iphis is in despair about her love, which she compares with the unnatural passion felt by Pasiphae for a bull (resulting in the birth of the Minotaur). Lamenting that "nature is unwilling" (758) to permit the longed-for marriage, she turns to the goddess Isis for help. The tale is finally brought to a happy conclusion when Isis remedies the mismatch between Iphis' desire and her gender by turning her into a boy.

Other writers suggested that a lesser metamorphosis might be involved. A fable by another Roman poet, Phaedrus, offers a solution to the question of what causes unusual desire in women and effeminacy or a desire to be sexually passive in men. The god Prometheus, who molded people out of clay, was working on a batch when he was invited to a party. He left his work and went out; by the time he returned home, he was so drunk that he stuck the men's genitals on the women and vice-versa (*Fables* 4.16). Although Phaedrus' explanation is humorous, the assumption underlying it is repeated in many other discussions: intercourse between women is repeatedly described in terms that denote physical penetration.

So Iphis attributes the prohibition on her love to nature, and Phaedrus explains its rare occurrence as a mistake in nature. But they both, in common with most of the Roman writers who mention it, manage simultaneously to lay its occurrence at the door of culture: Greek culture. Not only is Phaedrus' word for such abnormally mannish women a Greek one, *tribas,* meaning "one who rubs"; the figures in both his and Ovid's stories are Greek, and from the remote and mythical past to boot. The portrayal of Sappho in the *Heroides* also illustrates the Romans' habit of distancing themselves from female homoeroticism by seeing it as a Greek phenomenon.

Sappho herself does not appear in the most outrageous scenarios of tribadic love in Roman literature. Several epigrams by the poet Martial, for example, deal with tribads in vigorously insulting terms. One such (7.67) is addressed to a woman called Philaenis (she may be so named after the supposed author of a third century BCE Greek erotic handbook), whose sexual practices are dictated by the desire to be virile: so she sodomizes boys, penetrates eleven girls a day "with more fury than a stiffened husband," mud-wrestles, and vomits copiously after dinner. Martial mocks her aspirations (thereby, he hopes, proving himself a real man): she has it all wrong if she thinks cunnilingus is manly.

The fact that Martial restricts himself to calling Sappho merely "indecent" suggests that her status as a poet may have given her some protection. But this account of tribadism as ersatz virility clearly had an influence on how she was perceived. Horace in the first century BCE calls her "masculine Sappho" (*Epistles* 1.19; test. 34), and in the first century CE the poet Statius describes her suicidal plunge as " the manly leap / which Sappho fearlessly, recklessly, took from Leucas" (*Silvae* 5.3.154–155). Most important, this masculine aspect is echoed in the way she pursues both past and present loves in the *Heroides*. Phaon is explicitly described as the object of male desire, and Sappho as the older partner who desires him. As if to highlight the implications of this, Ovid includes a simile comparing her to a man: in order to persuade Sappho to follow her advice, the Naiad tells the (otherwise unknown) story of how Deucalion was cured of love for Pyrrha by his Leucadian leap. Sappho's love for the women of Leucas is much more lightly sketched, but here too she is the lover and they the beloved. In her active pursuit of both sexes we can now make out traces of the scandalous figure of the tribad, the woman who, like Martial's Philaenis, apes the man with both boys and girls.

Ovid's own relationship to this model is not straightforward: he has his own capital to make out of the ironies of gender reversal. But he is playing on a preoccupation with masculinity which was evidently even stronger among the Romans than the

Greeks, and which the discourse about tribads amply reveals. Sappho's fictional biography and Ovid's poem both derive some of their power to shock and to fascinate from the symbolic charge attached to masculinity in Roman culture. Roman manliness, asserted through an active sexual role, has connotations of vigor, power, military might; it is opposed to passivity, effeminacy, softness, and luxury. The figure of the tribad says far more about the need to maintain this opposition, and the dominance it shores up, than about contemporary sexual practice: witness the force of Martial's defense. The scandal of Sappho's sexuality is the threat it poses to this edifice.

## The Other Sappho

The last myth produced in antiquity about—or, in this case, not about—Sappho can be glimpsed only in a few relatively late sources, all of them Greek. But they are enough to suggest that this treatment of Greece's foremost woman writer caused concern. The problem was now ingeniously solved by suggesting that it was all a case of mistaken identity. There were two Sapphos, from two different towns in Lesbos; one was a poet and respectable, the other was neither. "I gather," says Aelian in the third century, "that there was in Lesbos another Sappho, a courtesan, not a poetess" (test. 4). Athenaeus around the beginning of that century adds one more detail: it was Sappho the courtesan who fell in love with Phaon (13.596e). Sappho's fictional erotic career was thus suppressed at a stroke, and this neat solution was obediently reproduced by the *Suda,* the encyclopedia quoted earlier. A second, shorter entry under the name of Sappho tells of *another* lyre player of the same name, who drowned for love of Phaon, and adds "some have said that she too composed lyric poetry" (test. 3). Even the uncertainty about Sappho's birthplace is turned to good account in this attempted whitewash: the poet Sappho was born in Eresus, whereas her disreputable namesake came from Mytilene.

Athenaeus attributes this information to a Syracusan writer of the fourth century BCE. So the story may have arisen first as a reaction to Sappho's portrayal in comedy, and there is no way of knowing how often it was referred to between then and Athenaeus' time. From the available sources it looks as if the revival of cultural nationalism among the Greeks of the second to fourth centuries led to a desire to rehabilitate Sappho, dissociating her from the disrepute into which Roman writers in particular had brought her.

It is striking, though, that these Greek sources do not make use of the myth of "the other" to defend Sappho against the charge of tribadism (and the main *Suda* entry reports her "bad reputation" without attempting to project it onto the Mytilenean Sappho). Once again, tribadism is of more concern to the Romans, and Sappho has her defenders here too. Writing in Latin, probably for school pupils, a third-century commentator on the Roman poet Horace, Porphyrio, tries to clarify what Horace might have meant by calling Sappho masculine. He concedes, though reluctantly, that tribadism is one possibility, speaking with the usual distaste of the "monstrous desire for intercourse with females" (commentary on Horace, *Epodes* 5.41). Porphyrio does not need to invoke the "other Sappho" in order to defend her. He has his own way out, though one that raises as many questions as it answers. The other explanation he offers for Horace's adjective, and one he clearly favors, is that she is famous for her poetry, "in which it is more often men who excel" (test. 17).

With his alternative explanations of Sappho's masculinity, Porphyrio brings together the two main strands of Sappho's mythical fortunes. Sappho the female poet or Sappho the sexual deviant? Perhaps the two were never very far apart. Each, after all, generated a myth as a defense against thinking the unthinkable. Sappho was not an outstanding female poet, she was a Muse; or she was not a sexual deviant, but the double of one. In both cases she inhabited the margins of what Greek, and then Roman, culture deemed acceptable—for a woman. It was no doubt this position on the margins that helped to give her image its phoenix-like powers of renewal.

# 2. Papyrus into Print

SOME SAPPHIC FICTIONS have little basis in her poetry, and some appropriate it for their own purposes. If we are to peel away some of the accretions of fantasy attached to her name, the obvious place to start would seem to be her own words. And we can lay hands on some respectably ancient source material: the oldest copy of a Sappho poem known to exist was made in the third century BCE, well before Ovid's imagination lit upon her.

Reading Sappho's own words, however, is not a simple process. There is, in the first place, the fact that so little of her poetic output survives. Only one of the surviving poems is complete, the famous ode to Aphrodite. Then there are perhaps ten poems of which we have a substantial part, followed by twenty or so quotations or fragments long enough for sustained interpretation. After that our texts degenerate into single lines or pairs of lines, halflines, and eventually single words.

The other complicating factor is the routes by which these fragments have traveled in the two and a half millennia since their composition. The remains of Sappho's poetry have reached the twentieth century in two forms. One is quotation by other ancient authors, many of them writing in the first few centuries CE and most with interests quite unrelated to hers. Snatches of Sappho's poems will be incorporated into a text by another author—perhaps a grammarian or an orator keen to display his erudition—whose work was copied sufficiently often to survive from antiquity up to the Renaissance and the advent of printing.

In the copying and recopying of manuscripts there is plenty of scope for error, and untangling it is a painstaking and uncertain process.

The other main source is texts written in antiquity on papyrus (the precursor of paper, made from reeds), which began to be discovered toward the end of the last century. The largest and most remarkable discovery was made at what used to be a town in Roman Egypt. The excavators of the site of ancient Oxyrhynchus (Town of the Sharp-Nosed Fish) uncovered what had been the town rubbish dump. The waste paper they discovered included, together with such everyday items as receipts, letters, and tax returns, a good deal of literature, in particular some previously unknown poetry of Sappho's. This kind of text presents the interpreter with another set of problems: flattening out fragile rolls or crumpled sheets, fitting torn fragments together, reading faded ink.

Let me try to illustrate what this means. If Hamlet's "To be or not to be" soliloquy in Shakespeare's play (act 3, scene 1) had survived only on a tattered scrap of third-century papyrus, it might look something like this when edited and printed:

]r n[o]t to be [....] i{s}s the quest[

?for ]her tis no[bl]er, in the mi[

]lings and arrows of [[cour]] 'outr'a[ge

]st a sea of trou[t

]nd them to die to sl[eep

The hypothetical papyrus on which this was written is eroded at the edges, so that the beginnings and ends of lines are now lost:

To be, or not to be, that is the question:
Whether 'tis nobler in the mind to suffer
The slings and arrows of outrageous fortune,
Or to take arms against a sea of troubles
And by opposing end them. To die—to sleep

*Papyrus into Print*

There is also damage within the surviving fragment, and such text as remains is presented with various shades of uncertainty, signaled by a battery of editorial markings: for example, a dot under an individual letter indicates that it is difficult to read and the editor cannot be sure it is correct. At the other extreme, some of this text is not by its original author at all: anything in square brackets is the editor's conjecture as to what might plausibly fill a gap. (For a list of these marks, see the Reading Notes.) In this case, as often, he has made several mistakes, the worst being the phrase "sea of trout" at a point where (we think) Shakespeare wrote "sea of trouble." Puzzling though it is, this would have seemed an obvious conjecture to an editor (what else would you find in a sea but fish?), and Shakespeare's version, even if it were proposed, would probably have been dismissed as too strained a metaphor. Still, with all of these efforts, we have only five lines of the speech.

If the editor of this poem were lucky, he might be able to put together with this papyrus fragment a few lines quoted from later in the speech by other writers. Perhaps a seventeenth-century essayist would be found who credited Hamlet in his famous speech of deliberation with the idea of death as an undiscovered country, and another who quoted the image directly: "the undiscovered country from which / No traveller returns." Much scholarly discussion would now follow because the second writer, no doubt quoting from memory like many ancient authors, has produced an unmetrical and therefore probably inaccurate line. At the end of this process, the following could be added to the first section of text:

death,

The undiscovered country from † which

No traveller returns

The dagger indicates a point at which the text is known to be corrupt but no one has come up with a plausible alternative. All

of this mirrors the way in which "the" text of Sappho is established.

There is no denying that the loss of so much of Sappho's
poetry is a serious one. But what remains is still enough to haunt
the imagination, to suggest a poet who is doing something subtle
and unusual with the traditions of her time. And the process by
which these texts have been transmitted and interpreted is in
itself fascinating. Sappho's poems cannot be completely insu-
lated from her fictional career. The cultures that spun fantasies
about her are also those that copied her texts, and as they did
so they stamped their preconceptions on them, whether by selection or by alteration. The same is true of even the most
scrupulous and scholarly modern texts. The copies we have
inherited, especially those on papyrus, are full of tantalizing
gaps, which have just as much power to seduce the reader into
fantasy as the most perfectly preserved love poems. Editors of
the poems, who consider it their job to reconstruct the text
wherever they can, are no more immune to their appeal than
anyone else; and almost all the poems I discuss later contain
supplements by editors. So the poems too have their fictional
aspect, and later I shall look in detail at some examples. First,
though, we should look at the fate of Sappho's texts during the
period separating her time from ours.

The circumstances in which Sappho's poems began their life are
shrouded in mystery and are linked with the key question of who
heard and performed them. By the same token, almost nothing
is known about how they were transmitted to begin with. It is
fairly certain, though, that they began not so much as literary
texts in our sense as songs, complete with melody and musical
accompaniment. It is more than likely that, for some time after
their composition, this was how many of her poems circulated.
As far as we know, writing was in only limited use in Sappho's
lifetime and for some time afterward; it was, on the other hand,
customary for at least the upper classes to be accomplished in

the art of music and to know a repertoire of songs by heart. A story recorded in the fifth century CE tells of a boy who sang one of Sappho's songs at a drinking party attended by the famous statesman Solon. Solon liked the song so much that he asked the boy, who was his nephew, to teach it to him; when asked why, he said, "So that I can learn it and then die!" (test. 10). Even if the anecdote is not based on fact, the scenario is plausible: there are plenty of other such stories about the work of famous poets.

But it seems unlikely that the bulk of Sappho's poetry was transmitted in this way for long, simply because there was so much of it (and unlike the much longer texts of Homer, her poems were neither full of repeated formulas nor memorized and performed by professional bards). Presumably, then, it was quite quickly written down. These early texts of Sappho may have taken some forms unfamiliar to us. Other poets of this period are said to have dedicated their poems in temples, in copies written in materials like lead or gold; since some of Sappho's poetry is devotional, she may well have done the same. Her poems could also have been used as reading and writing exercises when, probably shortly after her lifetime, literacy started to become a standard part of education: we might imagine generations of schoolchildren (girls as well as boys) learning to read aloud from texts of Sappho or laboriously incizing them on their own waxed writing tablets. But by the end of the fifth century, when there was an established book trade and a few rich individuals had begun to make collections of books, it is likely that Sappho's texts had found a more permanent form in what remained for some time the standard form of book: the papyrus roll. It is fitting, then, that portraits on vases eventually showed the poet herself reading. A water jug made in Athens in the second half of the fifth century has Sappho, identified by a name label, reading from one of these books, unrolling it with her right hand and rerolling it with her left (fig. 4).

Although they were important to the survival of Sappho's poetry, these early books were by no means the ideal medium for preserving it. They do not seem to have included musical notation, so that only words survived. Even worse, the texts were written in columns with no punctuation, no division between words, and no indication of the structure of the verse. Reading them must have been like reading Hamlet's speech as:

TOBEORNOTTO
BETHATISTHE
QUESTIONWHE
THERTISNOBL
ERINTHEMIND

Add to this the unwieldiness of the rolls themselves, and the experience of reading Sappho's songs in this form seems very remote from that of hearing or performing them.

From this point on, wherever the fate of Sappho's texts can be reconstructed, it seems increasingly to have been in the hands of commentators and antiquarians. Side by side with the biographical fictions we have surveyed, the fourth and third centuries BCE saw the beginning of a long tradition of scholarly commentary on her, discussing such things as the kind of the musical scales she used or her supposed invention of a kind of lyre. By far the most important scholarly activity of the period, though, was that of the librarians at Alexandria: without them we might well have had none of Sappho's poetry at all.

In the early third century, one of the successors of Alexander the Great founded, in the Egyptian city named after him, the Museum, or House of the Muses. The Museum included a library, which became the largest in the ancient world, and successive curators set themselves the task of making a complete collection of Greek literature. Texts were gathered from all sources and by any method: all ships docking in the city, for example, were searched for books. An anecdote about the plundering of Athens' archives illustrates the importance attached to the task. At the Athenians' request, the Alexandrians paid a deposit for the loan of the official copies of literary works owned by the city; once the books were in their hands, they decided to forfeit the deposit and sent back copies instead. After gathering their material, they then compared different versions and produced what were for most classical Greek authors the first standard texts, now complete with marginal signs to indicate layout and sometimes with editorial comments.

It was at this stage that Sappho was canonized as one of the nine great lyric poets. Her work was collected into nine books, divided according to the type of meter used; book 1 contained, we are told, as many as 1320 lines, in four-line stanzas, and another consisted entirely of songs written for wedding celebrations. It is this information about the Alexandrian edition above all which gives us the measure of how much Sappho was subsequently lost. There is no way of knowing for sure how this happened. Sappho's collected works, which seem to have been sufficiently important to go through two Alexandrian editions, were known for many centuries to come. Copies no doubt found their way into the other great libraries, such as the one set up to rival Alexandria's at Pergamum on what is now the Turkish coast, and private collectors must have continued making their own copies. When Roman poets and men of letters became interested in their Greek predecessors, Sappho's work was certainly available to them and they imitated her freely. Catullus in the first century BCE wrote imitations of her poems, and a little later in the century Sappho was among the Greek models used by Horace, especially for the stanza form named after her.

The Greek-speaking population of the Roman world also continued to value her poetry as part of their heritage, even if in a rather bookish way. During the Greek cultural revival of the second to fourth centuries, her songs were apparently sung, in time-honored fashion, after dinner (test. 53); but most of those who refer to her work sound as if they are working from texts. Longus, the author of a pastoral love story, builds into his text allusions to Sappho's poems which he obviously expects his educated readers to recognize. Two of her best-known poems had been studied in detail by Greek authors in the first centuries BCE and CE, and this tradition of learned commentary continued through the Roman Empire and into the Byzantine period. Many a scholar or antiquarian of the first few centuries CE will quote a line of Sappho to illustrate some abstruse point about grammar or vocabulary, thus incidentally preserving it in the only form that now exists, but obviously assuming that the text from which it is taken is accessible to his readers. And yet no manuscript of Sappho's complete works survived into the modern period.

Renaissance writers traced this loss to deliberate censorship by Christians. Petrus Alcyonius, for example, attributes to an earlier scholar the statement that not only Sappho's works but also those of several other dramatic and lyric poets were burned by Byzantine emperors at the instigation of the church, because they dealt with "the passions, obscenities and follies of lovers." But the main factor was probably much less dramatic than this. Lyric poets of Sappho's time whose work survived the first millennium in any quantity are the exception, not the rule, and much of what was lost does not fit this description. Like many of her contemporaries, Sappho probably just fell victim to a general narrowing of interest in the literature of the past, which resulted eventually in a drastic reduction in the number of classical texts in circulation.

It is not so much the loss of a classical author's work that requires explanation as its survival, and that depended largely on a continuing supply of readers interested enough to keep recopying it—still a laborious task in this preprinting era. But there are signs that Sappho was becoming a minority interest in the first few centuries CE, for a number of reasons. Perhaps the most important is the fashion, which took hold in the second century and lasted more or less throughout the Byzantine period, for writing Attic Greek, the dialect of classical Athens. It became mandatory to write in only one version of a language that had existed in many different dialect forms, and Sappho's Aeolic Greek was very different from the now dominant Attic version. The Roman writer Apuleius, who comments on the strangeness of her dialect (test. 48), was clearly not alone in finding it difficult to understand, as we can tell from the existence of several commentaries on it. A second factor was the growth of interest in rhetoric at the expense of poetry. It is true that tags from Sappho, as from other poets, were trotted out by aspiring orators as a badge of learning. But interest in archaic poetry for its own sake flagged, and many poets (with the notable exception of Homer) fell by the wayside. Finally, the spread of Christianity, though it may not have entailed active censorship, meant that people tended to stop reading pagan authors.

This powerful combination of factors may not have dealt an immediate death blow to Sappho's work, even in a period that saw the destruction of many library collections. It seems that at least some of her work survived two major changes in the technology of writing: the transition from papyrus to parchment as a writing material, and from the book roll to the codex, which was more like a modern book. From the second to the fourth centuries, the codex was gradually taking over from the roll as the standard format for literature. This would have been a particularly crucial period for the transmission of texts: authors whose work was not popular enough to be transcribed into codex form would tend to become less accessible to readers. The accompanying change, from papyrus to parchment, also has implications for survival because parchment, made of animal skins, is a superbly durable material and more likely to last through that period of decline in learning known as the Dark Ages. It is in fact just before the darkest period of all, the eighth century, that the latest copies we have of Sappho's poems were made, written on parchment codex pages in the sixth and seventh centuries. But here the trail of continuous transmission seems to go cold. Durable or not, these copies of Sappho, made for their own sake rather than to illustrate some point of debate, grammar, or dialect, have no successors.

The next moment of renewed interest in classical authors was the so-called Byzantine renaissance of the ninth century, when the scholars of Constantinople, like their Alexandrian predecessors, began making collections of ancient literature. Here another technological change intervened: the collections were transcribed into a new script, smaller and easier to write. Once again the new copies eventually superseded the old. This time, even if Sappho's texts still existed, there was clearly not enough interest to warrant their being transcribed. Some snippets of her work made their way into the anthologies and encyclopedias that are characteristic of the period, and learned references were still being made to her work. But by now the authors who quote her no longer give the impression that they have access to a larger body of material. The twelfth-century grammarian Tzetzes probably exaggerates only slightly when he mournfully declares that he will have to illustrate Sapphic meter from other poets' work, because "the passage of time has destroyed Sappho and her works, her lyre and her songs" (test. 61L).

This was not quite the end of Sappho. There were still texts by other authors containing excerpts from her poems—most only one or two lines long—as well as anthologies preserving a few of the Hellenistic epigrams that had been attributed to her. The survival of even these texts was by no means assured: toward its end the Byzantine empire, including its libraries, suffered increasingly at the hands of invaders, including the Crusaders who sacked Constantinople in 1204. Nonetheless, quite a number of the treatises and commentaries in which Sappho is quoted were among the manuscripts discovered by Renaissance collectors and eventually searched for their precious cargo of quotation. The early humanists had been more interested in Latin than in Greek, but by the fifteenth century knowledge of Greek was developing, and large numbers of Greek manuscripts were brought to Italy, either by refugees from the doomed Byzantine empire or by travelers who went in search of them.

In the sixteenth century, what remained of Sappho's work benefited from a technological advance that at last guaranteed the production of enough copies to ensure its survival: the printing press. Again things proceeded more slowly with Greek than with Latin, perhaps partly because of the greater difficulty of designing a typeface for the Greek script of the time. But from the late fifteenth century on, the work of getting the major Greek authors into print was being enthusiastically undertaken by scholar-printers, and among the newly printed works were some quoting Sappho. In 1508 one of the best-known of these early printers, Aldus Manutius in Venice, included three short works by Dionysius of Halicarnassus in a collection of Greek oratorical writings. Among them was the treatise *On Literary Composition,* which quotes the full text of an ode to Aphrodite. The treatise was then included in a more complete collection of Dionysius' works by the king's printer in Paris, Robert Estienne, in 1547. In these first printed copies, the ode is difficult to recognize as a poem because it is laid out in the same way as its prosaic surroundings, with only quotation marks to distinguish it from Dionysius' discussion of it. Seven years later, though, when Robert's son Henri Estienne added it to his edition of the lyric poet Anacreon, it appeared proudly in verse form under the name of Sappho (fig. 5). Similarly, Longinus' *On the Sublime,* first printed in 1554, included several stanzas of fragment 31, the poem addressed to a beloved woman; two years later it had been extracted from this context and added to the second edition of Henri Estienne's Anacreon.

It is still a moving experience to handle these precious early copies of the surviving remnants of Sappho and other poets of her time, and to sense the excitement of rediscovering their work, even if the process also gave rise to a certain amount of competitive showmanship on the part of scholars and printers. In Sappho's case, the excitement was all the greater because her high reputation went before her. In the same year that Longinus was first published in full, Marc-Antoine de Muret printed the text of fragment 31 as part of his commentary on Catullus, because it was the model for Catullus' most famous imitation (poem 51) of Sappho. But Muret obviously finds the Sapphic original at least as interesting as its Latin successor. Evidently unaware that his thunder has already been stolen, he relates with relish his discovery of "the verses of a woman who far excelled all other poets in human history in this genre" and introduces the text itself with the words, "And now I think there is no one who is not impatient to listen to the tenth Muse."

The process of continuing discovery and examination of Sapphic fragments can be traced quite clearly in Henri Estienne's collected edition of the nine lyric poets, the first with any claim to being comprehensive as far as Sappho is concerned. For the first edition, published in 1560, Estienne evidently made a search of many sources, most of which quote only a line or two from Sappho. One of them is Athenaeus, who wrote his compendious collection of anecdotes and gossip about 200 CE; it was published in Venice as early as 1514. Estienne sets out the resulting fragments as verse, with a facing Latin translation (which sometimes gives out). But before the book reached its final form, he seems to have made more discoveries, including some previously unnoticed quotations in Athenaeus. These he adds at the end in a different format, with no translation but this time with some of the surrounding text. The most striking feature of these late additions is the fact that they are quoted as if they were prose. Neither Estienne nor anyone else has yet established the correct metrical divisions, and in an afterword addressed to his learned readers he both apologizes for any omissions they may find and bequeaths to them the work on meter that remains to be done.

By the time the work reached its second edition, six years later, he had more sources to add and was branching out to include quotations about as well as by Sappho. One of the effects of this is that Sappho's texts are sandwiched between accounts of her life that contain a good deal of fiction. In both editions, the poetry was prefaced by a life of Sappho excerpted from an Italian humanist, Giraldi, whose encyclopedic work on ancient poets' lives was published in 1545. Giraldi's sources include recent as well as ancient commentators on Sappho, and he often passes some comment on their reliability. It is all the more striking, therefore, that several details about her scandalous sexuality creep in that he neither dismisses nor attributes to a source. As well as giving one new twist to the story—it was only after her husband's death that she "burned shamelessly for boys and girls alike"—Giraldi also betrays the influence of Ovid when he reports that Sappho fell in love first with girls and then with "the

adolescent Phaon." Ovid's influence was consolidated in Estienne's 1566 edition, at the end of which epistle 15 of the *Heroides* was printed in full. Within six years of its first appearance, then, the first modern collection of Sappho's poems was equipped with an Ovidian filter.

But the texts had also entered a new phase in their preservation. Once the major texts were in print, their survival was a much less precarious affair, even if it was often overshadowed by Sappho's career in fiction. All the editions mentioned above exist today in the British Library and many other collections. Not all of Henri Estienne's successors followed his example of combing a wide range of sources for the most modest of quotations. There were subsequent editions in which the number of poems quoted was actually reduced, and the two major poems mentioned above were often the only ones known to the reading public. But there were no further major threats to survival. By the late nineteenth century, thanks especially to continuing scholarly activity in Germany, the number of fragments of Sappho printed in collections had increased more than fourfold. In addition, systematic work on the manuscripts and language of the poems had produced a relatively stable text in place of the wildly differing variants printed in the early editions.

The last phase in the reconstitution of Sappho's work as we have it, the excavation of texts written on papyrus, takes the narrative both on to the 1890s and back to the ancient world. In the second half of the nineteenth century, as the cultivation of land in Egypt expanded, an increasing number of ancient papyrus texts, preserved in the dry ground, were being found and eventually sold on the antiquities market. These papyri aroused great interest among western scholars. But there was also concern about the destruction of papyri by inexpert excavators and at the way finds were split up for sale, so that their origins remained unknown. Various western countries therefore began to mount expeditions to Egypt to search for papyri. Among them was Britain, where the traditions of classical education for the upper classes ensured a public willing to contribute funds.

The excavators of Oxyrhynchus, now called Behnesa, were two young men from Oxford University. Bernard Grenfell and Arthur Hunt made their first visit to Egypt on behalf of the London-based Egypt Exploration Fund in 1895. A year later they selected a promising site 120 miles south of Cairo, and they began early in 1897 to dig trenches into a series of low mounds. Almost immediately they met with spectacular success. The mounds turned out to be heaps of ancient rubbish, and in Grenfell's words "the flow of papyri soon became a torrent it was difficult to keep pace with." Over a hundred local workers had to be employed, working an eleven-hour day, and the supply of containers was soon outstripped.

In a play by Tony Harrison, *The Trackers of Oxyrhynchus*, Grenfell and Hunt are shown by their tents after a day's excavation, rummaging through their spoils in search of something interesting:

GRENFELL    God, I do wish some
            *literature* would come to light.
            Petition, petition, receipt, receipt.
            Orders for the payment of supplies of wheat . . .

HUNT        Petitions, petitions, receipts and leases.
            Can't call these finds lost masterpieces.

Most of the material did indeed consist of roll after roll of the documents of everyday life, sometimes dumped on the rubbish heap by the basketful. Material of this kind is now more highly valued as a historical source, but at the time it was the scarce literary and religious texts that were the focus of attention. The greatest stir was created by a single page, apparently of sayings of Jesus, which was reported with great excitement at the Egypt Exploration Fund's annual meeting later that year. But there was also a copy, made in the third century CE, of a previously un-known poem by Sappho about her brother. Grenfell and Hunt included it in their first published volume of Oxyrhynchus pa-pyri, but the general scarcity of literary material led them to remark, "it is not very likely that we shall find another poem of Sappho."

Happily they were wrong. Their work in Egypt continued, and in 1906 they wrote to the London *Times* announcing another literary find and appealing for donations. Instead of the usual batches of documents, they had come across the remains of two private libraries. Of the second, they write:

> about 8 feet from the surface, we came upon a thin layer which throughout an area of many square yards was full of literary fragments, while stray pieces belonging to the same texts were found some distance away. The evidence of documents found below the literary texts shows that the latter must have been thrown away in the fifth century [CE]; but the manuscripts themselves are chiefly of the second or third century . . . It is doubtful whether continuous sheets of much length can be built up out of the innumerable fragments, which range in size from some lines to a few letters. This is the more regrettable because the owner of the library was much interested in the lyric poets. His collection included two or three manuscripts apparently of Sappho.
>
> (*Times*, May 14, 1906)

It was this cache that provided the bulk of the Sappho papyrus texts, the largest new collection for several centuries. Paradoxi-cally enough, those who threw their copies away in the fifth century contributed more to the poems' survival than many others who took better care of them.

This period, during which so many ancient texts were redis-covered, seemed like a second Renaissance for the scholarly world: one of those involved writes of "an ideal time" in which "we lived over again the days of the Renaissance." Like the first Renaissance, it generated an immense editing task, involving many more people than the original excavators. The processing of the Oxyrhynchus material has continued long after the deaths of Grenfell and Hunt. The sixtieth volume was published in 1993, and there are still crates of unprocessed fragments in the basement of the Ashmolean Museum at Oxford.

Can we hope that more Sappho will be discovered? The unedited Oxyrhynchus papyri are not a likely source because the collection has been combed for literary material. But similar collections exist elsewhere, such as the finds of an American excavation carried out in Egypt in the 1920s and only partially published, which are now at the University of Michigan. The area around Oxyrhynchus is no longer promising because of irrigation work, resulting in a level of ground humidity that will destroy any remaining papyrus. As Harrison's Grenfell puts it, "Spinach now flourishes from the pulped-up roll / that held still hidden secrets of Sappho's soul." But manuscripts are still coming to light elsewhere. A relatively small-scale excavation was begun in the 1980s of what was evidently an important urban center in the western Sahara, occupied in the first few centuries CE. The site, in the Dakhleh peninsula, has already yielded some papyrus fragments, found in houses together with pots and other domestic objects. Among the most important finds so far, though, are two books made of sewn-together wooden boards; one contains accounts, but the other is a literary text, the work of the classical Athenian orator Isocrates. Similar discoveries of Sappho cannot be ruled out: her "white, speaking columns," as a Hellenistic poet called them (test. 15), may have more to say to us yet.

## The Poems

I shall now try to fill in this outline by looking at some poems that have survived into the twentieth century. All but one are fragments, not complete poems, and often the gaps occur throughout the text, not just at its beginning or end. I quote the poems here in the plain prose translation of the Loeb edition, with breaks added to indicate stanza ends (a later chapter will consider some verse renderings) and with gaps and reconstructions indicated.

### ODE TO APHRODITE (POEM 1)

Ornate-throned immortal Aphrodite, wile-weaving daughter of Zeus, I entreat you: do not overpower my heart, mistress, with ache and anguish,

but come here, if ever in the past you heard my voice from afar and acquiesced and came, leaving your father's golden house,

with chariot yoked: beautiful swift sparrows whirring fast-beating wings brought you above the dark earth down from heaven through the mid-air,

and soon they arrived; and you, blessed one, with a smile on your immortal face asked what was the matter with me this time and why I was calling this time

and what in my maddened heart I most wished to happen for myself: 'Whom am I to persuade this time to lead you back to her love? Who wrongs you, Sappho?

If she runs away, soon she shall pursue; if she does not accept gifts, why, she shall give them instead; and if she does not love, soon she shall love even against her will.'

Come to me now again and deliver me from oppressive anxieties; fulfil all that my heart longs to fulfil, and you yourself be my fellow-fighter.

This famous poem is still the only complete one of Sappho's in existence, and it owes its survival to the treatise on literary composition mentioned earlier. The author is Dionysius, an orator and historian who came from Halicarnassus (now Bodrum, in Turkey) but lived and wrote in Rome from about 30 BCE. He chooses Sappho as one of his examples of the "polished or exuberant" style, and quotes the poem in full before going on to a detailed analysis of its "euphony and charm." Some scraps also exist on a papyrus from Oxyrhynchus and in other authors' quotations; but Dionysius, whose own work survived in a direct manuscript tradition, is the only source for most of it.

But if this poem has fared uniquely well in terms of transmission, it also illustrates in a remarkable way the problems that can arise through centuries of recopying. There are a number of points in the text at which the surviving manuscripts (of which there are many) give different readings of the same passage. None is more intriguing, though, than the passage translated as "even against her will." In the Greek this is the only point in the poem at which it is made explicit that the speaker's beloved is a woman, not a man; and this in a poem that, unusually, names Sappho herself as the speaker. So this looks like a crucial piece of evidence about Sappho's sexuality. But the text at just this point is hopelessly garbled.

The manuscripts on which modern texts are based give three variants, none of which can be correct because none both makes sense and fits the dialect and meter (a Sapphic stanza, described in Chapter 5)—and this includes the one variant that makes the beloved female. What is an editor to do? The early printed texts gave several different versions, all of which can now be seen on metrical grounds to be wrong. They also, without exception, sidestepped the gender problem. Estienne, for example, printed a version meaning something like "whatever you command" and left the beloved's gender unspecified. But the ambiguity was not reproduced by translators and interpreters of the poem, who until the nineteenth century tended overwhelmingly to assume that this was a poem about heterosexual love.

Despite advances in the understanding of meter, the currently accepted reading of the single word in question was not proposed until 1835, by the German editor Theodor Bergk. His emendation of the word, which makes the beloved female, stays fairly close to the manuscript versions. The basis of his later defense, though, is not within the text but outside it. In first proposing the reading he asserts simply that "we are dealing with the love of a *girl*"; then he is forced by hostile criticism to defend his judgment. At this point we can see that his main piece of evidence is not new: on the contrary, it had been available since the Renaissance. Apart from a line in Horace and Sappho's supposed rejection of Alcaeus' love, Bergk relies on Sappho's other poems to show that "she had a strong aversion to the love of men" and passionately sought female friendship. This argument owes as much to contemporary assumptions—about poetry as autobiography, about the incompatibility of homosexual and heterosexual love—as it does to technical detail; and yet there is no way of resolving the difficulties without making such assumptions. The vagaries, or perhaps worse, of manuscript tradition have left us, at this crucial point in the text, not with certainties but with a conundrum.

### HERODIAN ON CUSHIONS (FRAGMENT 46)

[Let us return to the matter under discussion, namely *tulē*, cushion, which was not used by the Attic writers but is used by Sappho in book 2.]

and I will lay down my limbs on soft cushions.

This snatch of quotation, which appears in a treatise of the second century CE entitled *On Anomalous Words,* is far more representative of the Sapphic manuscript tradition than the ode to Aphrodite. It also illustrates the antiquarian interests that led many writers of the time to Sappho. Its author, Herodian, lived in Rome; he was a grammarian and the son of an equally famous scholar from Alexandria. Both father and son quote snippets from Sappho, including some from the ode to Aphrodite, in the course of erudite discussions of matters such as Greek dialects, grammar, and meter; here what interests Herodian is one word alone. In this case no fuller quotation has come to light, and so we are left with this single, tantalizing phrase, extracted from Herodian's work by Renaissance printers. With no information at all about the line—who is the speaker, for example?—its significance, as opposed to its bare meaning, is virtually impossible to assess.

OLD AGE? (FRAGMENT 18, SAPPHO OR ALCAEUS)

   . . . the moon was coming into view

   . . . both distress and health

   . . . children, I might flee . . .; youth

Like the Herodian extract, this has survived partly because it is quoted by another writer, this time a metrician whose name is unknown. Our source for it, however, is older: it was unearthed at Oxyrhynchus, written on papyrus that goes back to the second century. It is elegantly written and well laid out, and was probably a private copy made by a scholar for his own use.

Many of the difficulties of interpreting papyrus texts are illustrated here. First, only a handful of words survive. As often, the task of piecing the text together is made somewhat easier by the fact that the reverse side of the fragment has been used for another text, a commentary on Homer; only if both sides fit together can a reading be correct. Then there is the problem of attribution: this author's interest is in meter, so he quotes from a wide range of poets without identifying them. The dialect of the fragment is enough to identify this as the work of Sappho or Alcaeus, though one word has been written in its Attic form, which would have been more familiar to the scribe. One line alone can be matched with another quotation: the first is cited by yet another metrician, who also identifies it as Sappho's (154). But this does not help with the remaining two lines, which do not follow on from it. The best we can say is that it may be about old age, a subject common in lyric poetry and treated by both Sappho and Alcaeus.

[S]ome say a host of cavalry, others of infantry, and others of ships, [i]s the most beautiful thing o[n] the bla[c]k earth, but I say it is whatsoever a person loves.

It is [per]fectly easy to make th[i]s understood by [ev]eryone: for she who far surpassed [ma]nkind in beauty, Helen, l[eft] her most [noble] husband

and went sail[ing] off to Troy with no thought [at all] for her [ch]ild or dear pa[r]ents, but [love] led her astray . . .

. . . lightly [and she] has [r]emin[ded] me now of Anactori[a] who is [not] here;

I would rather see h[er] lovely walk and the bright sparkle of her face than the Lydians' chariots and armed [infantry]

. . . impossible to happen
. . . manki[nd] . . . but to pray to [s]hare

(9 lines missing)

unexpectedl[y]

As the many gaps suggest, this too is a text preserved on papyrus at Oxyrhynchus (fig. 6). But here we have one of the main prizes of the 1906 find. Good fortune has yielded a collection of fragments that have, with a good deal of industry and ingenuity, been shown to come from a single poem, one of the most fascinating of Sappho's to survive. The text is based on no fewer than twenty separate pieces of papyrus; a single line is also quoted in a second-century treatise on syntax. The copy from which the papyrus fragments came was probably made for the book trade, also in the second century, and has some quite sophisticated editorial markings (some added by a second scribe) to indicate such things as meter and the divisions between poems. Even so, it must have been quite difficult to read, written as it is without even word divisions. Probably because of this and because of the unfamiliarity of the dialect, the scribe who added the metrical markings got several of them wrong.

The process by which this poem was gradually pieced together is a good example of how hazardous the reconstruction of a text from papyrus can be. Before the assembly of the latest scraps, there were even more gaps than there are now, and scholars were not slow to try and fill them. In the first edition of the poem Grenfell and Hunt, making what appeared to be some reasonable guesses about what was in the gaps in front of them, produced the following version of Helen's actions in the second and third stanzas: "Helen judged him [Paris] best who destroyed the majesty of Troy." Another tiny papyrus scrap, when fitted into place, showed how wrong this version was. The lines actually refer to Helen's own journey to Troy: far from admiring masculine heroism, she abandons it (in the person of Menelaus) to sail for Troy herself. This makes of Helen a far more interesting and subversive figure, and accentuates the poem's ironic perspective on traditional military values. In cases like this, where we can check editors' reconstructions against later finds, the reconstructions often turn out to be wrong: in this case, and perhaps not accidentally, Sappho's male editors also took a more conservative line than she had about women's relation to men. On such fragile foundations is built our understanding of her work.

PARTING (FRAGMENT 94)

. . . and honestly I wish I were dead. She was leaving me with many tears

and said this: Oh what bad luck has be[en] ours, Sappho; truly I leave you against my will.

I replied to her thus: Go and fare well and remember me, for you know how we cared for you.

If not, why then I want to remind you . . . and the good times we had.

You put on m[any wreath]s of violets and ro[ses] and
[cro]cuses together . . . by my side,

and [round your t]ender neck you [put] m[any] wov[en
gar]lands made from flowers

and . . . with much flowery perfume . . . [fit for a qu]een,
you anointed [yourself]

and [o]n soft beds . . . you would satisfy [your] longin[g for]
tender . . .

There was neither . . . [n]or shrine . . . from whi[ch w]e
were absent,

no grove . . . [nor d]ance . . . sound

This poem, one of four places where Sappho's own name appears in her poetry, survives in a copy made just before the loss
of her work in the Dark Ages. It was not in Oxyrhynchus but in
a collection that probably came from the same part of the world
and is now in Berlin. Written on parchment, the text comes from
a book, not a roll; like all the texts discussed so far, it has no
word divisions. Again there is some overlap with two short (and
rather garbled) quotations in another author, Athenaeus. In this
text, like the last, there are problems of interpretation at key
points. In ancient literary texts, other than dramatic ones, there
is no way of indicating a change of speaker, so we do not know
which of the two women is speaking the opening words (which
in any case are not the beginning of the poem). It is beyond
doubt here that two women are involved, but controversy has
focused on the question of what word comes immediately after
the phrase "you would satisfy [your] longing for." Who or what
comes next? This time the corruption of the manuscript cannot
be attributed to human intervention, simply to time. The ink
happens to have faded at a crucial point, but we can just make
out the traces of a word that *might* read "young girls," and
would produce either the phrase "you satisfied your desire for
young girls" or "you satisfied the desire of young girls": that is,

your own. The first of these translations might support the argument that relationships between older and younger women were usual in Sappho's circle. But as so often with Sappho, we cannot be sure.

PRAYER FOR APHRODITE'S PRESENCE (FRAGMENT 2)

*Coming down from . . .*

Hither to me from Crete t[o this] holy temple, wher[e] is [your] delightful grove o[f] apple-trees, and altars smoking with [i]ncense;

therein cold water babbles through apple-branches, and the whole place is shadowed by roses, and from the shimmering leaves the sleep of enchantment comes down;

therein too a meadow, where horses graze, blossoms with spring flowers, and the winds blow gently . . .

there . . . Cypris, take and pour gracefully into golden cups nectar that is mingled with our festivities.

From one of the latest surviving texts of Sappho, we come here to one of the earliest. There are a few short and inaccurate quotations from this prayer to Aphrodite in other authors, but the fullest version of the text is one of the two oldest known copies of a Sapphic poem, and it is written on a material unique in our collection: a piece of broken terracotta pottery. It was found in Egypt and can now be seen at the Biblioteca Laurenziana in Florence, cradled in velvet like a holy relic.

The style of the handwriting indicates that this copy dates from the mid third or second century BCE; not so easy to establish is why the copy was made and why this material was used. Potsherds were, as far as we know, generally used for ephemeral purposes: as cloakroom tickets in the baths, for example, or ration tokens for quarry workers. The text itself also presents a puzzle: the quality of the writing is that of an experienced scribe, but he has made so many mistakes that his text in places makes no sense.

Two suggestions have been made as to the origins of this text: that it is the private copy of a poetry enthusiast who was unfamiliar with the dialect in which Sappho wrote, or that it was produced in a school context. In favor of the second hypothesis is the fact that, although literature was normally written on papyrus, it was also sometimes copied out onto potsherds for educational use: so this copy might be the work of a schoolmaster. Whatever the truth of this, it is alarming to find so many errors in a text that is one of the earliest copies of Sappho we possess.

The opening words (in italics) also throw up an enigma to which no satisfactory answer has been found. Though damaged, they evidently formed part of the first line written on the sherd; but they do not fit the meter of the rest of the poem, and a new stanza begins just after them. So it has been suggested that this was one of a set of sherds and that these words are the end of a previous poem. Although this produces an unusually abrupt-sounding invocation, no better solution has suggested itself, so the text of the poem is normally taken as starting with the words "Hither to me."

In addition to the material on which it is written, there is another respect in which this fragment is unique among texts of Sappho. It did not appear in print until 1937, when it was published by an Italian papyrologist called Medea Norsa, the only woman to have edited Sappho and still one of very few to follow that line of work. Since 1971 the main scholarly edition of Sappho's collected texts has been that of a woman, Eva-Maria Voigt—but the fate of Sappho's surviving words, as of her reputation, has still been overwhelmingly in the hands of men.

To point this out is not to suggest that the gender of the editor automatically shapes each individual text. But the fact that women do not figure in the history of Sappho's texts before the twentieth century is a reminder that their survival, as well as being random, has also been highly determined. The hands through which the poems have passed have all left their imprints, of which editorial judgments are only the most visible. At each stage of the poems' survival, it is possible to trace the influence of contemporary assumptions and institutions, just as we could in Sappho's fictional career: assumptions about gender figure in both. And yet to wish away the poems' posterity would be to wish them lost again and to deny the patience, skill, and industry that have gone into their preservation.

It would also be to deny a process of which we ourselves are part. The point was deftly made by Ezra Pound, who in 1916 published a poem he called "Papyrus":

Spring . . . . . .

Too long . . . . . .

Gongula . . . . . .

Pound's poem, inspired by some just-published scraps of Sappho, would have been better entitled "Parchment," since the Sapphic fragments on which it is based come from an early edition of another Berlin parchment (95), but that is hardly the point. Pound's poem was part of the development of a poetics to which fragmentariness was central: partly inspired by the manuscript finds, modernist poems also helped to create the poetic taste through which their contents could be read. In an extended sense, this too has helped to constitute the collection of Sappho accessible to twentieth-century readers, and is part of the process that makes her poems legible. Greek texts are habitually printed with an array of footnotes about disputed details, including the names of editors who have proposed particular variants, and for Sappho's fragments the notes often include the brief but telling statement that a particular editor "recreated" *(refinxit)* this version. It is not only the interpretation of her life that has its creative aspect.

# 3. Poetry and Politics

THE FORTUNES OF SAPPHO in later antiquity re-solved themselves into two parallel but distinct strands, accord-ing to which she was either a poet of mythical powers or a sexual deviant. In this chapter and the next I take these two images in turn and consider each in the context of Sappho's own time. The main question inspiring this chapter arises from her repre-sentation as a Muse: goddesses aside, what were the circum-stances in which a real woman could compose poetry in the seventh and sixth centuries BCE?

It is clear that there was already a strong tradition of poetic composition on the island of Lesbos. A line by Sappho herself boasts of how superior Lesbian singers were to those from other lands (106), and both history and myth seem to bear her out. Lesbos' unique association with poetry is represented in myth by the story of the poet Orpheus, whose severed head was thrown into a river by the women who had killed him; eventually, still singing, it floated over the sea to Lesbos and was buried there. The distinguished singers the island produced in historical times include Sappho's male contemporary Alcaeus, as well as two others thought to have lived earlier in the seventh century BCE. Terpander was credited with the invention of the drinking song, as well as with increasing the number of lyre strings from four to seven; later in the century came Arion, who was said to have been the first composer of the dithyramb, a type of song performed by a chorus. Arion was also famous for having been miraculously rescued from death, in a story recounted by Herodotus in the fifth century BCE (1.23). When the crew of a ship on which he was traveling to Corinth decided to steal his money and drown him, Arion asked to be allowed to sing one last song. "Delighted at the prospect of hearing a song from the world's most famous singer," the murderous sailors agreed, and Arion, arrayed in his singer's robes, stood on deck and sang, accompanying himself on the lyre. As soon as the song was over he jumped into the sea, but a dolphin carried him safely back to land on its back. The story illustrates not only the international celebrity status that poets might acquire, but also their semi-magical powers: like prophets, they all had something of the divine about them.

But all these poets are men. Though tradition has preserved the names of a few female poets from early Greece, almost nothing is known of them or their work, and none apart from Sappho is connected with Lesbos. Helena, Manto, and Phantasia, said to have been precursors even of Homer, are shadowy figures whose names are linked with those of other figures from myth. In the later archaic period, Megalostrata of Sparta can at least be related to a known historical person, the poet Alcman, but only through a story of the familiar type concerning his love for her. None of this is of any help in understanding the real conditions of poetic composition by women.

There are a number of other reasons why this question cannot be approached directly. As these stories show, poetry in the archaic period was primarily a performance art, and figures like Sappho were more like the singer-songwriters of today than the poets. Since their work always required an audience, the situations for which they wrote were all to some extent public. The question of how Sappho came to be a poet, then, leads to wider questions about the social life and structures of her time, especially those involving women.

The trouble is that, for the time and place we are dealing with, such questions are extremely difficult to answer. The sources for any history of the Greek world in Sappho's lifetime are notoriously sparse: for her native island of Lesbos, her own poetry and that of Alcaeus are the most substantial we have. Even when we move on to the classical period and to the much better-documented city of Athens, there is still little of the kind of information on which modern social history is based: we have, for example, no statistical information and no private documents such as letters or diaries. And despite the fact that records for classical Athens are better than for anywhere else in the period, not a single female poet is recorded as having composed there.

Thus I have been forced to look well beyond Sappho's own time and place in the search for material with which to make sense of her role as woman and poet. Some of my discussion depends partly on written sources from many centuries after her lifetime, even from as late as the Byzantine period; the *Suda* entry from the tenth century helps to illustrate the biases and omissions that can arise. A redeeming factor here, though, is that historians have been able to consider these sources alongside other kinds of material, especially archeological findings.

We also find ourselves often faced with images rather than realities. Much of the source material dating from Sappho's time or thereabouts is either literary or artistic: the Homeric poems, say, or representations of women on vases. Neither can be looked to in any simple way for information about real life. Both are produced for particular kinds of occasion and audience, which largely dictate their content, and both deal in idealized images, within artistic traditions that do not pretend to be realistic. The Homeric poems create a world in which ships are swift, the sea wine-dark, and every dawn rosy-fingered. The fact that in this world women are often described as white-armed says little about real women's lives, and far more about what was expected of women (some at least) in the culture.

But culturally determined perceptions of this kind can still help to provide a context both for Sappho's role and for the poetic traditions of her time. Bearing these limitations in mind, I begin with a brief account of Lesbos in the archaic period.

## Archaic Lesbos

By far the largest of the Aegean islands (with an area of some 630 square miles), Lesbos in the seventh and sixth centuries BCE was situated on the eastern fringes of the Greek-speaking world. About 100 miles away to the west and southwest was the coast of mainland Greece; immediately to the north and east lay Anatolia (Turkey), dominated by the non-Greek kingdom of Lydia; to the south were the Ionian Greek islands and coastal cities such as Ephesus and Miletus.

Some aspects of the life and culture of Lesbos at this time, the style of its wall-building for example, were unique to the island. But it was also part of a much wider network. Its closest neighbors, both geographically and culturally, were the small Greek settlements on the nearby Anatolian coast, many of them dependencies of Lesbian cities. There were also connections with mainland Greece. Tradition had it that Lesbos' original colonizers came from northern Greece, and the Aeolic dialect spoken in both places showed the affinity. During Sappho's lifetime there was also conflict with mainland Greece, when a Lesbian army fought Athenian settlers for possession of Sigeum, a key site on the shipping route to the Black Sea. And the island had cultural and political interests in common with the Ionian Greeks to the south, as well as links with non-Greek areas farther afield.

The period was one of great change, and Greek cities were being forced to expand their horizons. For reasons not fully understood, many Greek cities were sending out expeditions to colonize non-Greek areas and to establish Greek cities, sometimes as far away as modern Spain or France (Marseilles, then called Massilia, was one such colony). This activity was in full swing in Sappho's lifetime, and though not one of the foremost colonizers, Lesbos too was part of it, helping to found a new city to the north in Thrace and others closer to home.

At the same time, there was an expansion of trading activity, in which Lesbos once again played a part. By the end of the seventh century, trade with Egypt had grown sufficiently to warrant the establishment of a Greek trading post in the Nile delta, called Naucratis (which like Oxyrhynchus was a site of excavation in the nineteenth century, though the discoveries were of pottery and inscriptions, not papyrus). According to Herodotus, Sappho's own brother was among those who traveled to Egypt (2.135), and a later source, Strabo, adds the information that he was exporting wine to Naucratis (202). Another important center lay to the east: the aggressively expansionist kingdom of Lydia, as well as intermittently coming into conflict with Greek settlements, also traded with them. Linked to the spread of trade is the use of coinage, thought to have been invented in Lydia in or near Sappho's lifetime.

Internal changes were also taking place in Greek cities. The basic political unit of the time was the polis, an independent community based on a relatively small area of agricultural land and with an urban center: Athens, with its surrounding territory of Attica, later became the most famous example, though its size makes it untypical. On Lesbos the most powerful polis was Mytilene, one of the two cities later reputed to be Sappho's birthplace, which for generations had been ruled by the Penthilidai, a dynasty tracing its descent from the legendary Penthilus, son of Orestes. But in this climate of economic and social change, the supremacy of the established aristocracy was being challenged throughout the Greek world, and Mytilene was no exception.

Sappho's lifetime coincided with one of the city's most turbulent periods, whose details are reconstructed mainly through the poetry of Alcaeus. The overthrow of the Penthilidai was followed by a power struggle between several aristocratic families; and, as in other cities, there was a rapid succession of tyrants (meaning, here, nonlegitimate rulers) drawn from these families. The involvement of Alcaeus' family began, as far as we know, when his two brothers joined with another aristocrat, Pittacus, to oust the tyrant Melanchrous. Alcaeus himself later conspired with Pittacus against another tyrant, Myrsilus. But Pittacus betrayed his oath and changed sides, and Alcaeus was forced into exile, railing bitterly against his former ally. Alcaeus remained on the losing side when, after Myrsilus' death, Pittacus himself came to power. It is a sign of the changing times that he did so not only with the support of a few aristocratic conspirators, but by the will of the wider populace, who are said to have elected him for a ten-year period.

Much of Alcaeus' poetry is concerned with this aristocratic plotting and counterplotting, and Sappho too must have been affected by it. It is certain that she came from an aristocratic family herself, and an inscription on marble from the island of Paros records that she fled from Mytilene to Sicily some time between 605 and 590 BCE; the reason is not stated, but was probably political. Yet political preoccupations do not take the same form in her poetry as in Alcaeus'. In order to see why, we need to look at the occasions for which poetry was composed.

## Poetry and Performance

Poetry in early Greece was very different from what goes under that name today, most obviously because it was composed not to be read but to be heard. It was a branch not of literature but of music, or *mousikē* (the art of the Muses), which included instrumental playing, dance, and song. The occasions on which music might be called for embraced all aspects and stages of life.

Many such occasions are described in the earliest works of Greek literature known to us, the Homeric epics; perhaps not surprisingly, it is the performance of epic poetry itself that appears most often. Two separate stages of Odysseus' wanderings include accounts of the singing of bards. When he arrives in the land of the Phaeacians, their king Alcinous welcomes him with a feast. As part of the preparations, the bard Demodocus is summoned, and after the meal he sings to the assembled company: "the Muse roused the singer to sing the praises of men, a lay whose fame reached to the broad heaven, the quarrel between Odysseus and Achilles" (*Odyssey* 8.73–5, tr. Barker). Demodocus' song could be an extract from the kind of poem within which he himself figures. Like the epic poet, he sings of the heroic deeds of those who fought at Troy, and he too is regarded as divinely inspired. Later in the *Odyssey* we meet another bard, Phemius, who is described in similar terms. The epic tradition probably goes back to these tales of heroic glory sung at feasts by professional singers.

Other kinds of musicmaking appear in the epics, linked with particular occasions such as weddings and funerals. In book 18 of the *Iliad* the blacksmith god Hephaestus forges for Achilles a new shield on which are represented scenes from everyday life, described in loving detail by the poet. One shows wedding processions, with brides being escorted through the streets to their new husbands' homes. Song, instrumental music, and dance are all involved:

> they were leading the brides from their houses through the town with blazing torches, and a loud wedding song rose up. Young men whirled in the dance, while among them *auloi* [pipes] and *phorminges* [lyres] gave forth their voice; and the women stood in the doorway admiring the sight.
> (*Iliad* 18.492–496, tr. Barker)

The *Odyssey* includes a brief glimpse of another stage of marriage, the wedding party. On his return home, Odysseus kills his wife's suitors and, in order to cover up the mayhem that follows, gives orders for a fake wedding party. This time the bard takes the lead, but his task here is not just to entertain a listening audience: it is to play his lyre and sing while leading the entire company in a dance, so that "the great house resounded to the feet of the merrily dancing men and the beautifully dressed women" (23.146–147).

Funerals also involve both specialist musicians and others. The last book of the *Iliad* describes the Trojans' mourning for Hector, led first by professional male singers and then by, in turn, Hector's wife, mother, and sister-in-law. Each sings an individual lament, which is answered by all the other women; and at the climax all the "countless people" moan in response (24.776).

Many other less formal occasions include song and dance. Addresses to the gods, whether planned or spontaneous, are sung: the Greeks sing paeans to Apollo both to ask for deliverance from plague and, later, in thanks for victory over Hector. The shield of Achilles shows other peacetime scenes involving music, such as a harvest scene in which youths and maidens carry baskets of grapes. As the work proceeds, a boy in their midst plays the lyre and sings a traditional lament for the mythical figure of Linus; others follow him, stamping time to the music and singing. The next scene has groups of young men and maidens performing a round dance and probably singing. This time it is not a singer who leads the dance but two acrobats, who "whirled in the midst of them" (*Iliad* 18.606).

These epic scenes, depicting ordinary people as well as professional musicians, show music interwoven with everyday life. They also illustrate the different forms it can take, from unison singing and dancing at one extreme to solo song with lyre accompaniment at the other, and sometimes a combination of both. With few exceptions, however, it is a communal activity. When Achilles withdraws from the fighting and sits alone with his lyre singing of "the famous deeds of men" (*Iliad* 9.189), his solitary celebration of the ideals he shares with other heroes serves only to accentuate his isolation at this point in the poem.

The picture painted in the epics, though idealized, is borne out by other sources from the centuries following their composition. Vase illustrations often show a dancing chorus led by a lyre player, just as these passages describe. We also have a body of poetry from this period, representing the words—all that survives—of the songs. Most of this is, like Sappho's, by famous named poets and has been preserved for that reason. Like her work too, it is mostly fragmentary, but enough survives to show affinities with the musicmaking described in epic. These shorter poems include hymns to gods, laments, and wedding songs; and they too make liberal use of myth, telling and retelling the stories of heroes of old.

But there are some differences. The most important is the appearance among the poems surviving from this period of a more personal-sounding kind of poetry, evidently intended for solo performance. The singer in many of these shorter poems tells not, like Achilles, of the men of old, but of the brevity of life's pleasures, of youth, beauty, wine, and love. It was these apparently more intimate poems that led eventually to the association of lyric with the private and the personal; and some of them do contain allusions to events and people who were part of the poets' lives and, presumably, known to their audiences. For a long time it was customary to interpret all these songs as containing autobiographical confessions about the poet's life. But the poems probably have both as much and as little association with the poets' lives as those of modern singers, drawing on their composer's experience and milieu but not always representing it directly. And as with our songs, the subject matter falls within a defined range dictated partly by the expectations of the audience.

The second important difference between the poetry described in epic and that of Sappho's time has, in fact, to do with its audience. The society depicted in the Homeric poems is dominated by a small group of heroes who stand out from other men because of their physical beauty and martial prowess. These qualities, emblematic of high social status, are emphasized by the epithet attached to each name: Menelaus of the loud war cry, swift-footed Achilles, godlike Diomedes. It is this small group of leaders, together with their households, followers, and guests, who form the audiences for bards like Demodocus and Phemius. Throughout the poems we come across them feasting together in gatherings composed mainly of men, though women are sometimes described as coming down from their quarters when the meal is over and the singing begins. Their sumptuous hospitality served a clearly defined purpose: to consolidate both the heroes' bonds with one another and their status as warriors within the community. The poet of the *Iliad* spells out the significance of feasts in book 12, when he has one hero, Sarpedon, explain to another that the luxury they enjoy at feasts is a sign of their favored status within their community, granted in recognition of their willingness to risk their lives in battle for their fellow Lycians (310–328).

But by the time of Sappho, although the practice of eating and drinking together persisted, its significance had changed. Success in warfare depended (as perhaps it always had) on disciplined groups of fighters rather than individuals, and political power was becoming more widely spread; as a result, the image of the heroic aristocratic warrior became more difficult to sustain. The successor to the warrior feast in the archaic period was the symposium, an exclusively male drinking party that now resembled an aristocratic club, concerned to defend both its exclusivity and its power against outsiders. It also provided an audience that, more than any other, shaped the lyric poetry of the time.

## Poetry at the Symposium

There is an evocative description of the beginning of one of these drinking parties in a poem by Xenophanes, a poet who wrote somewhat later than Sappho:

> Now the floor is swept, our hands are washed
>   and the cups clean. A servant garlands us;
> another brings round perfume in a dish.
>   The mixing bowl stands full of merriment;
> more wine is ready in jars, flower-scented,
>   gentle, promising not to fail us.
> Frankincense wafts a holy fragrance in our midst;
>   the water is cool and sweet and pure
> (1)

Xenophanes goes on to describe the opening ceremonies, hymns and wine offerings to the gods, after which the drinking and the entertainment begin. A favorite entertainment was singing, but this time by the participants themselves, not by a professional bard. One or more of the feasters, accompanied by either wind instrument or lyre, would sing from an existing repertoire or impromptu; and here Xenophanes makes a recommendation that clearly reflects the broader purposes of these meetings. A singer should, he says, expound great deeds, to remind his audience of excellence and encourage them to strive for it: he should, that is, hold up to the aristocratic symposiasts a mirror to reflect and promote the qualities that justify their social preeminence.

Most of the work of Sappho's contemporary Alcaeus was composed for gatherings like these. Many of his poems (which, like Sappho's, survive only in fragments) concentrate on the delights of convivial drinking. In one, he urges his friend Melanippus to enjoy life's pleasures while he may, using an example from myth to argue that drinking days will be over all too soon:

> Drink and be merry with me, Melanippus. You don't think that, once over the great whirling river of
>
> Death, you'll ever see the sun's clear light again? That's too much to hope.
>
> Look at Sisyphus, Aeolus' son, a king unmatched in cunning: he thought he could outwit death,
>
> but for all his wiles Fate made him cross that river again, and Zeus son of Cronus planned
>
> hard labour for him under the dark earth
> (38a)

Many of his other poems, though they do not allude to the symposium, were no doubt destined to be sung to his drinking companions. Later writers tell us that he dealt with the favorite sympotic theme of love, writing poems to beloved boys, though little of them survives. There are also short and apparently free-standing mythical narratives, telling a familiar story from a new angle, and hymns to deities. In a hymn calling on the twin gods Castor and Pollux, Alcaeus draws on an age-old formula when he reminds them of the powers from which he hopes to benefit:

> you who roam the whole wide earth
> and all the sea on swift horses,
> easily rescuing men
>   from chilly death;
>
> you leap to the tops of sturdy vessels,
> and as you dart up the ropes, you shine out
> and in the perilous dark bring light
>   to a black ship.
>   (34.5–12)

This plea to the patron saints of seafarers would be of special interest to Alcaeus' island-dwelling companions, and their common life informs his work in other ways too. A poem about the hall in which they feasted evokes their comradeship in arms in a Homeric-sounding description of the weaponry stacked up in it: plumed helmets, greaves, corslets, shields, swords (140). Elsewhere Alcaeus apparently welcomed his brother back from war, celebrating a feat of single combat of which any Homeric warrior might be proud. The poem is paraphrased by a later author: "According to Alcaeus, his brother performed a great feat while fighting as an ally of the Babylonians, and rescued them from trouble by killing a warrior who was over eight feet tall" (350). Despite its apparently personal content, a poem like this one, harking back to the good old days of heroic achievement, represents an ideal shared by aristocratic poet and audience.

But it is Alcaeus' political poems that are most clearly marked by the setting in which they were sung. He tells us more about historical figures like Pittacus and Myrsilus than any other writer, and the reason is that his listeners are also fellow conspirators. His poems do not simply reflect political intrigue: they are one of the ways of engaging in it. When Myrsilus dies, Alcaeus enlists his friends and allies in the celebration:

72

> Now is the time for every man
> to drink and get drunk with all his might:
> Myrsilus is dead!
>   (332)

And when Pittacus reneges on the oaths they had sworn together, Alcaeus vilifies him in song, whipping up his friends' thirst for vengeance with a litany of insults. Among them are some that harp on Pittacus' lack of true blue blood: the fact that he had a Thracian mother enables Alcaeus and his friends to stigmatize him as "base-born," reflecting their sense of threat from new social groupings.

Although references to contemporary politics are not completely absent from Sappho's poetry, they are far fewer and less direct. Respectable women were generally excluded from male gatherings and from the world of war. Sappho's songs, and those of other unrecorded women poets, must have been performed in other social settings, many of which were for women only and reflected the social roles allotted to them. Of these, the single most important is that of bride.

## Marriage in Archaic Greece

Both the Homeric epics and Alcaeus' poetry make it clear that the destiny of a male aristocrat was to become a warrior. A woman of noble birth was supposed to aspire to a quite different end: to marry. The sources focus particularly on women at the stage of their lives leading up to marriage, reflecting not so much their own life experience as the crucial importance of marriage to aristocratic society as a whole.

A short poem by Alcaeus, apparently complete, shows clearly what kind of woman was officially acceptable. It begins with an address to Helen, the woman whose "bad deeds" brought death and destruction to Priam of Troy and his sons. But the rest of the poem focuses on a contrasting figure:

> Not so was the bride the son of Aeacus took:
> he summoned the blessed gods to the wedding
> and led from the halls of [her father] Nereus
>    the delicate maiden,
>
> and took her to Cheiron's home. There
> he loosened the pure maiden's girdle.
> The love of Peleus and the best of Nereids flourished,
>    and within a year
>
> she bore a son, finest of demigods,
> blessed driver of golden stallions.
> But through Helen, the Trojans perished
>    and all their city.
>   (42)

73

The contrast between Helen and Thetis, bride of Peleus, works on several levels. Thetis is twice described with a word reserved for a young woman as yet unmarried, *parthenos* (plural *parthenoi*), or a maiden. This marks her off clearly from Helen, a sexually mature woman notorious for her adultery with Paris, which caused the Trojan war. Later in the poem, when Thetis becomes a mother, another contrast comes into play. Thetis' son is Achilles, "the finest of demigods, blessed driver of golden stallions"; Helen's child is a daughter, absent from this poem and rarely mentioned elsewhere, who could never rival the achievement of Achilles. The fact that Achilles was also involved in destroying Troy is a contradiction that the poem glosses over.

The role of the virtuous woman is clear: to be a pure bride and then the mother of legitimate warrior sons, inheritors of the family name, wealth, and glory. And the focus is on transactions between men, with Thetis playing only a passive part. Both she and Peleus are identified with reference to their fathers, stressing their noble birth within a patrilineal society. The two men also take the initiative: Peleus summons the wedding guests, takes

Thetis from her father's house to his own, and takes the sexual initiative ("he loosened the pure maiden's girdle"); Nereus will have given his daughter in marriage.

Many of these details are echoed elsewhere. As in the wedding scene from the *Iliad,* it was the bride, taken from her father's home to her husband's, for whom marriage involved the greatest upheaval (fig. 7). The Homeric poems also demonstrate the importance of marriage as a means of alliance between aristocratic families. The high value placed on women in these exchanges is represented in both *Iliad* and *Odyssey* by the giving of bridewealth, a gift from the groom's family to the bride's rather than, as with a dowry, the other way around. Although bridewealth was not current in Sappho's time, aristocratic marriage was still a cornerstone of social and political relations. Melas, tyrant of Ephesus, is among those known to have made use of it in this period, marrying a daughter of the king of Lydia; their son succeeded him as ruler, which suggests that the move was successful in consolidating the Ephesian dynasty's position both inside and outside the city. The same maneuver was practiced by Pittacus when he married into the Penthilidai, the original ruling family of Mytilene: Alcaeus mentions it in poem 70, with a bitterness that shows how effective the strategy was.

The fact that marriage was used to form alliances between aristocratic dynasties, and Alcaeus' corresponding portrayal of the ideal bride, does not necessarily tell us much about the participants' experience of it. Sappho's poetry suggests that love and marriage can be viewed in a very different way, and the condition of parthenos occupied only a small part of a woman's life, unlike the comparable status for a man, that of citizen and fighter, which lasted until he reached old age. But the social importance of marriage had a determining effect in two important areas: the way women are represented in literary and artistic sources, and the opportunities they themselves had to participate in *mousikē.* It helps to explain why images of young women are so widespread, and why beauty and grace receive such emphasis in descriptions of them. Second, marriage and preparation for marriage are among the occasions that call for women themselves, and thus potentially women poets, to engage in song and dance.

## Women and Music

The two descriptions of weddings from the Homeric poems both include women among the participants: as spectators of the procession and as dancers at the party. Two other accounts of weddings give them an even more prominent role. A scene in the *Shield of Heracles* (280), a poem written in imitation of the Homeric description of Achilles' shield, shows a bride being taken to her husband in a cart: maidservants carrying torches head the procession, which also includes a female chorus "dancing a lovely dance to the sound of lyres" (fig. 8). And in a fragment of narrative by Sappho written, unusually for her, in epic style and language, women have an even larger part to play.

The subject is the marriage of the Trojan prince Hector to Andromache, and the surviving section opens with a herald's announcement that Hector and his companions are bringing Andromache to Troy from her home in Thebe. As the news spreads through the city, women and girls are among those who set out to join in the celebrations, and the girls take a prominent role in the musicmaking that follows:

> the sweet-sounding pipe and cithara [lyre] were mingled
> and the sound of castanets, and maidens [parthenoi]
> sang clearly a holy song, and a marvellous echo
> reached the sky
> (44L, 24–27)

At the close of the poem the older women raise a cry of joy, while the men sing a paean to Apollo, god of the lyre.

These scenes share an important feature with the others described earlier. Even when men and women are shown together, it is usual for them to be separated into groups according to both gender and status. Not only are the two sexes normally segregated: boys are distinguished from adult men, and girls from women. At Hector's funeral, it is specifically the married women who lament, whereas in the dancing scene represented on Achilles' shield the dancers, both male and female, are young. This picture echoes other sources in showing a society in which social roles, including gender roles, are very sharply differentiated, and different sexes and age groups spend much of their time apart.

The care with which these divisions are specified also helps to highlight the prominence of groups who share the status of Thetis in Alcaeus' poem, that of parthenos. Time and again in myth, literature, and the visual arts we encounter groups of girls on the verge of womanhood, and the surrounding narratives show that there is a strong link between membership in such a group and the stage of life just before marriage. In the *Odyssey* the Phaeacian princess Nausicaa, whose thoughts when we first meet her are turning to marriage, is playing a kind of dancing ballgame with her attendants when Odysseus comes upon her, and the situation itself is one of the ways in which the narrative hints at a romantic attachment. And in the dancing scene from the *Iliad,* the poet makes the maidens' status clear when he describes them as "bringing in oxen" (593), that is, liable to be wooed by suitors who will offer valuable bridegifts.

Two features recur regularly in these scenes. The girls' beauty and grace both reflect and idealize their marriageable state; and these qualities are characteristically expressed in choral singing and dancing. Myth too provides images of young women so engaged: the Muses and the Graces symbolize poetry and beauty respectively and are themselves represented as parthenoi. A Homeric hymn to Apollo, for example, shows his arrival on Mount Olympus, greeted by the singing of the Muses and the dancing of the Graces, and in the eighth century Hesiod begins his long poem about the genealogy of the gods with an invocation to the Muses, who live on the great and holy mountain of Helicon, and dance with their tender feet around the violet-coloured spring and the altar of [Zeus]. When they have washed their soft bodies . . . they begin to make their beautiful, lovely dances on the top of Helicon, stepping strongly with their feet. From there they fly up, covered in a thick mist, and go about in the night, singing with most beautiful voices, hymning Zeus the aegis-bearer.

(*Theogony* 2-11, tr. Barker)

It is undoubtedly the social and symbolic importance of this stage of life that explains why it is so frequently represented. But there is reason to think that in some parts of the Greek world the social reality corresponded to the representation, and that for young women and young men alike, the approach to adulthood was negotiated through a period of quasi-initiation. Both would participate in rites of passage that took place through the worship, and under the protection, of an appropriate deity. And for both, but especially for girls, singing and dancing played an important part (fig. 9).

A clearer idea of some of the activities of these groups of adolescents can be gleaned from the work of Alcman, a poet who wrote, probably a little earlier than Sappho, in Sparta. Sparta's educational system, which later became famous throughout the Greek world, involved for both boys and girls a period of segregation from the rest of society in single-sex groups, and Alcman's surviving poems, all fragmentary, include some written to be sung and danced by such groups. Those for which he became best known, and of which most survives, are the songs written for choruses of girls and collected by the Alexandrian editors under the title *partheneia*, maiden songs.

A later commentator, whose work survives on papyrus, puts an important slant on Alcman's role in relation to these choruses, describing him as "trainer of [the Spartans'] daughters and young men in traditional choruses" (test. 9). Although this statement comes from a later period, it is confirmed by what we know of Alcman's time. The poetry already quoted here deals with idealized social roles and behavior, and even in Plato, over two centuries later, choral dancing was recognized as central to the educational process. It is natural that it should have been a way of transmitting traditional values to the young, and that Alcman's role as a poet should include educating the girls who performed his works.

It is unlikely that his contribution was limited to providing words and music. The musicmaking scenes just considered include several examples of bards who sing and play while also leading the dance, as well as choral songs led by individual singers; illustrations on vases often show dancers led by musicians. Several of the surviving fragments, it is true, make reference to a chorus leader chosen from among the dancers themselves: in the longest of the partheneia fragments, the chorus sing the praises of a girl whose name, Hagesichora, means "leader of the chorus" (1), and elsewhere a corresponding male figure, a beardless youth called Hagesidamos, "leader of the people," is mentioned (10a). In another fragment, though, an older male singer addresses to parthenoi a lament about the infirmity of age:

> Oh honey-tongued, holy-voiced girls, my limbs
> will no longer carry me. If only I were a kingfisher,
> flying over the flower of the wave with the halcyon-birds
> with fearless heart, a strong, sea-blue bird.
> (26)

The third-century BCE writer who quotes these words adds an explanation: Alcman, he says, was unable because of his age to "whirl about with the choirs and the girls' dancing." Before age overtook him, then, this is exactly what the poet would be expected to do, and even after that he probably taught by example, perhaps setting the music in motion with an invocation like this: "Come Muse, clear-voiced Muse of many songs, singer always, begin a new song for girls to sing" (14L), and then accompanying it on his lyre. It is possible that Sappho sometimes played a comparable role for the aristocratic maidens of Lesbos.

## Sappho as Poet

The circumstances for which Sappho's poems were composed have long been a matter of controversy. There are no contempo- rary accounts, like Xenophanes' poem about symposia, to tell us about gatherings of women, and no other female poets from the period whose work might provide clues. Apart from later sources, then, we have little except Sappho's own poems to use in trying to answer this all-important question.

One theory sees Sappho as a kind of priestess, presiding over a religious group for which she composed devotional songs, and some support for this view can be found in her poetry. Many of her songs have a devotional aspect, and in some cases they can even be linked with known festivals or cults. One snatch of song seems to have been composed for the Adonia. A soloist and chorus, apparently singing in alternation, represent the goddess Aphrodite and her worshippers lamenting the death of her beloved Adonis:

> "Gentle Adonis is dying, Cytherea: what shall we do?"
> "Beat your breasts, maidens, and tear your clothes."
>   (140a)

And among Sappho's many hymns is one addressed to Hera, thought to be part of a trinity of gods worshipped at a cult center on Lesbos.

But the presence of a religious element in her work is not enough to make of her a priestess. Prayer and worship were a regular part of life for both sexes, and while there were few established priesthoods at this time, almost all poets of the period composed songs to gods. By no means were these all performed in cult situations. Xenophanes' poem shows that symposia routinely began with prayer, and Alcaeus' poems, sung to his drinking companions, include some calling on the gods for help against enemies. It is likely that, as well as composing for festivals and ceremonies, Sappho too addressed the gods in song on less formal occasions.

*Poetry and Politics*

Another theory links Sappho's work with the kind of girls' choruses for which Alcman wrote. According to this view, Sappho too is to be thought of as leading groups of parthenoi in the manner described for Alcman, and several later sources back up the parallel by allotting her an explicitly educational role. The *Suda* entry, for example, mentions by name three female "pupils" from other parts of Anatolia, and a fragmentary commentary preserved on papyrus from the second century CE speaks of her as "educating nobly-born girls, not only from local families but also from families in Ionia" (214b). But these statements have one problematic aspect. Although young men might travel long distances from their home cities in order to be educated, there is no evidence from anywhere else in the Greek world that young women did too. Like the image of Sappho as priestess, this view probably reads back into her life the authority she later acquired, representing her poetic influence in the form of a direct relationship.

At the same time, though, there is quite a bit of evidence to support the idea of a link between Sappho's poetry and parthenoi. Her usual audience is female: fragment 160 announces the singer's intention to "delight my companions" with songs, using the feminine form of the word "companion." And although Sappho's Greek often indicates no more than gender, several poems specify that the status of the female figures mentioned is that of parthenos. This is especially true of the poems composed for performance at weddings, which seem to have made up an entire book in the Alexandrian edition of her work. In the fragments we have, there are several references to the bride's virgin status, and one even has the bride herself singing in dialogue with her virginity:

"Maidenhood, maidenhood, where have you gone, deserting me?"
"Never again shall I come to you: never again."
(114)

The celebrants at weddings also, as in the narrative about Hector and Andromache, included groups of girls who would accompany the procession to the groom's house and even as far as the bridal chamber. The surviving fragments of songs composed for them by Sappho, written in a simple, folksong style, include not only complimentary addresses to the bride and groom but also playful mockery of the doorkeeper who stands guard to prevent the bride's friends from rescuing her:

> The doorkeeper's feet are seven fathoms long
> and his sandals are made from five ox-hides;
> it took ten cobblers to make them.
> (110a)

Outside the context of weddings, the term *parthenos* appears less often, but it is still found, and several other features of Sappho's poems suggest a focus on this stage of life. As in Alcman, there are calls for the presence of both Muses and Graces. Hera, addressed in fragment 17, presides over marriage and time of life just before it, while Aphrodite, the goddess most frequently invoked in Sappho, symbolizes and bestows the attractiveness required in a bride. Many of the activities described in the poems are designed to enhance female accomplishment and charm: one fragment commends a parthenos for her skill, probably in music (56), while another refers disparagingly to someone ignorant of proper dress (57).

Another aspect of the poems suggesting a link with young women is the frequent reference to partings and absence. One of the longer fragments (96) refers to a former companion who is now gone. She is far away "among the women of Lydia"; even so, declares the poet, she still remembers and longs for her beloved Atthis. In a society that practiced patrilocal marriage, the most plausible reason for women to travel such distances was to be married, and the description of Atthis' friend contains a hint that this is indeed the reason for their separation: her companions in Lydia are no longer girls on the threshold of adult status, but women.

Finally, there are some similarities of language and imagery between Sappho and Alcman, and even fragments of her work (21, 58) which, like lines from Alcman, suggest an older singer performing in concert with young female dancers. The image of Sappho as the leader of young dancers or celebrants is taken up by several later writers, who picture her surrounded by groups of parthenoi (test. 21; Philostratus, *Imagines* 2.1; Himerius, *Speeches* 9).

Although most of this evidence is circumstantial, it does lend considerable weight to the idea that Sappho's work was connected with, and important for, groups of young women. To be a parthenos was to be at the prime of life, the moment when a woman was most highly valued by her culture. It is natural that a female poet, working within an idealizing poetic tradition, should celebrate it in song, just as male poets sang of heroic warrior figures. It is beyond doubt too that some of her songs were composed for parthenoi, and performing them would have been important in training these young women in the roles expected of them.

In a play written in the late fifth century by Euripides, a group of women cast their thoughts nostalgically back to their youth. Singing in unison, they long for a return to earlier, happier times:

> I wish . . . that I could stand in the dance-choruses at noble weddings, as, when I was a girl, I whirled near my mother's feet in the joyful bands of my young friends, entering the contests of the Graces, the rivalry of our rich, soft hair, and shadowing my face with scarves, intricately adorned, and with my flowing locks.
>
> (*Iphigenia among the Taurians* 1143–52, tr. Barker)

There are many echoes here of situations evoked in Sappho's poetry. Groups of young girls dance together, sometimes at weddings, invoke the Graces as patrons, and take pride in elaborate adornment. Even the rivalry mentioned can be paralleled from

Sappho's time: a poem by Alcaeus tells of a sacred place where the female inhabitants of Lesbos "go to and fro with trailing robes being judged for beauty, and around rings the marvellous sound of the sacred yearly shout of women" (130b). Even though Euripides is writing two centuries after Sappho, it may not be too fanciful to imagine that the shared life of parthenoi on Lesbos included similar activities.

Again, though, it is unlikely that Sappho's role was limited to that of mentor in the way later tradition suggests. For one thing, she may herself have composed at different stages of her life, and for different groups at different times. Many of her poems are certainly for girls, but others are said by the authors who quote them to be addressed to adult women, *gynaikes* (55, 193). At least one fragment seems to be addressed by an older woman to a companion of her youth (24), while in another a girl sings to her mother (102). The fact that some of the fragments probably have fictional contexts serves only to complicate the picture.

Later in life as an established poet, Sappho may well have overseen the training of young choruses: Euripides' chorus remember dancing under a mother's eye, and there are several examples from other parts of the Greek world of older women supervising the initiatory activities of the young. Perhaps too, like Alcman, she sometimes led them herself in the way pictured by a later poet:

> Come to the sacred precinct of bull-faced Hera,
> you dwellers on Lesbos, whirling your delicate footsteps,
> and there set up a beautiful dance to the goddess; and
> Sappho will lead you, her golden lyre in her hand.
> Happy you dancers in the delightful dancing! Indeed
> you will think you hear a sweet song from Calliope herself.
> (*Greek Anthology* 9.189; test. 59)

But there were surely also times, such as the annual festival described by Alcaeus, when Sappho's companions in worship included other adult women.

It is clear too that Sappho's is not the only voice we hear in her poetry. Even the solo songs for which she became best known often point to the presence of other virtuoso musicians among her listeners. Although Sappho herself and those connected with her, such as her brothers, are occasionally named within the poems, so too are a host of other female figures some of whom also sing and play the lyre. Fragment 21 invites an unnamed female singer to "sing to us of the violet-robed [Aphrodite]," probably accompanying herself on the lyre; in fragment 22 the subject of a similar song is the beauty of a third female figure. On these less formal-sounding occasions, her fellow singers may well have included girls and older women together, perhaps continuing to practice the arts they had learned as girls in all-female gatherings of a kind later depicted on classical Athenian vases.

Our knowledge of the circumstances in which Sappho sang will always be sketchy. But we shall probably do best to imagine her making music on many occasions, both formal and informal, in the shared life of girls and women. There is good reason to think that religious ritual and the initiation of maidens both figured prominently among the occasions that brought them together. But to see Sappho only as a priestess or only as an educator is to misrepresent the rich variety of her work. It is also to overlook another equally important dimension of her musicmaking.

## Sappho's World

Although the world of Sappho's poems is mainly female, it is not a sequestered world. The story of her exile, if true, indicates that she was a figure of some social prominence, and her poetry provides evidence of involvement in the wider world of Lesbian and even international affairs. I have stressed the importance of marriage in aristocratic social relations, and there are other ways in which her poetry represents an aristocratic world view. There is, for example, no trace of the misogyny found in some other archaic poets. Apart from the obvious fact that she is herself a woman, this can be linked with her membership in a class for whom women are an asset. By contrast, peasant farmers such as those for whom Hesiod wrote his *Works and Days,* a compendium of agricultural and general advice, regard women as a necessary evil, who if they give birth to too many hungry mouths will wreck the family economy. Thus in Hesiod female beauty, as shown in the myth of Pandora, is a snare, not something to be celebrated.

Beauty in girls and women was also part of a specifically aristocratic ideal of accomplishment, as we can see from its negative portrayal in the seventh-century poet Semonides. Writing from a perspective similar to Hesiod's, he lists types of women created from animals. The results are hardly flattering. The sow-woman keeps a disorderly and dirty house and is herself unwashed, while the ass-woman works only under compulsion, never stops eating, and will accept any sexual partner. The woman "created from a dainty mare" is also criticized for her reluctance to work: instead she spends all day washing herself and putting on perfume and flowers. Her social class is clear not only from her parentage—horses were a luxury of the upper classes—but also from the poet's closing remarks: this woman, he says, is a bane to her husband unless he is a tyrant or king (7.57–70).

Sappho's poetry, by contrast, shows how the cultivation of beauty in women corresponds to martial prowess in men. A paraphrase of one of her wedding songs indicates that as well as comparing the bride to a sweet apple on the topmost bough, ready to be picked, her poem also "likened the bridegroom to Achilles, and put the young man on a par with the hero in his achievements" (105b). In common with the image of male heroism, idealized female beauty underpins high social status. Moreover, the few nonaristocratic women who figure in her poetry are treated quite differently. The girl who does not know "how to pull her rags over her ankles" (57) is also described as "rustic." These phrases are said to come from a poem mocking Andromeda, who is bewitched by the girl; and it may well be that the mockery arises from a connection inappropriate to Andromeda's rank. Similarly, when the addressee of fragment 55 is criticized for her lack of skill, her failing is no doubt social as much as personal:

> . . . when you die you will lie there, and no-one will ever
> remember or long for you later. For you have no share
> of Pierian roses: so when gone from here,
> invisible even in Hades, you will flit to and fro with the
> shadowy dead.

Plutarch, who quotes these lines, tells us that they were addressed to a woman who was uncultured and ignorant but also wealthy. If poetic skill was a badge of social accomplishment for aristocratic women as it certainly was for men, then this poem may be as intimately bound up in the politics of Lesbos as any of Alcaeus' tirades, pitting aristocratic culture against mere wealth.

Issues about aristocratic honor and its relation to wealth are in fact explicitly addressed elsewhere in Sappho, as in many of the male poets of this period. Alcaeus quotes a sage's saying that "no poor man is good or honourable" (360); Sappho says that the combination of wealth and excellence is the height of happiness (148). Elsewhere she expresses concern for family honor in a poem (5) about her brother Charaxus. Praying that he will redeem former mistakes, she sets out a model of behavior that any aristocrat from Homer on would recognize: he should be a joy to his friends and a bane to his enemies. That this is a public aspiration, and not one peculiar to Sappho, is suggested both by the mention of citizens later in the poem (though in a context too damaged for precise interpretation) and by the very fact that the poem was composed for performance.

Other references to people and places reach out to a world beyond Sappho's immediate surroundings, and even beyond her island. There are contacts with the nearby mainland: an address to Aphrodite mentions cloth sent as an offering by a woman from Phocaea, on the Anatolian coast south of Lesbos (101), and we are told that Sappho referred to the nearby promontory of Aega (170). But perhaps the most significant references are to Lydia and its capital city, Sardis. Lydia is both the source of fine clothing and an emblem of riches, used in two poems to express an individual's value to the speaker: "I would not [take] all Lydia in exchange for her" (132, 16). It is also the place where Atthis' former companion now "stands out among the women." This poem points to a role for Sappho and her "servants of the Muses" in relations between Lesbos and Lydia. Alcaeus tells of intervention by Lydia in Lesbian politics, and earlier I referred to the Lydian royal family's intermarriage with the ruling dynasty at Ephesus: the marriage of Atthis' friend was probably part of this process of forging international links between noble families.

The evidence for Sappho's involvement in the internal politics of Lesbos is even clearer. Commentaries on Alcman's poetry written in the first and second centuries CE indicate that the choruses for which he wrote were identified with particular localities and tribal groupings in Sparta. In Sappho's case there seem to have been links with the aristocratic families who are also encountered in the poetry of Alcaeus: the exile of Myrsilus' family, the Cleanactidai, is mentioned (98b), as is Lesbos' former ruling dynasty, the Penthilidai (71). So it is likely that both she and her audience were, like Alcaeus, positioned within the power struggles of the time.

One possibility as to the form her involvement took is suggested by Maximus of Tyre, who writes in the second century CE that Sappho, like the Athenian Socrates, had two rivals. Of Socrates' relationship with other teachers, who also attracted a following among the young, he says: "what the rival practitioners Prodicus and Gorgias and Protagoras were to Socrates, Gorgo and Andromeda were to Sappho" (test. 20). These names, both female, are mentioned in Sappho's poetry in contexts that are consistent with Maximus' interpretation. In one fragment Atthis is said to be "flying off to Andromeda" (131); another seems to refer to people who "have had quite enough of Gorgo" (144). Maximus continues with a quotation implying that both are members of the Polyanactid ("much-ruling") family, an otherwise unknown family mentioned several times in Sappho (99a, 155, 213a).

This may be the key to their relationship with Sappho. Another fragment addresses a girl or woman called Mica and continues, "you chose the friendship of the female Penthilidai" (71). The evidence is so fragmentary that we cannot be certain, but it looks as if many of the attachments and rivalries in her poetry may have arisen from those of the families concerned. Even the ways in which both she and Alcaeus retell traditional stories may have political resonances. Penthilus, the ancestor of the Penthilidai, was the son of Orestes and the grandson of Agamemnon. This means that the Trojan war is part of their family history, which can be told in ways either subtly complimentary to them or the reverse. Competing versions of what we would regard as myths could certainly have political consequences: in the conflict over Sigeum, both the Athenians and their Lesbian opponents used events in the Trojan war to back up their claims.

Even though we cannot reconstruct all the detail, it is clear that both the composition and the survival of Sappho's poetry depended on her social milieu. Her membership in the aristocracy is the single most important factor. As the rest of Semonides' poem shows in its preoccupation with work, only aristocratic women would have had the leisure for extensive musicmaking or the status to ensure that their work was valued and preserved. In a culture so imbued with *mousikē*, women from other social groups must have participated in it, but we have only one tantalizing glimpse of their activity. A song that the philosopher Thales, from Miletus, reported hearing sung by a woman on Lesbos indicates just as much involvement in politics as Sappho's poetry, but unlike hers it is accompanied by the manual labor that would have been the lot of most women:

Grind, mill, grind:
for even Pittacus grinds,
the ruler of great Mytilene.
(869)

It was also aristocratic values and social relations that placed
Sappho's companions, and her poetry, under the patronage of
those two sets of divine parthenoi, the Muses and the Graces.
Yet there is another divinity central to Sappho's work who is by
no means a maiden: Aphrodite. The role of the goddess of desire
and the eroticism of so many songs lead us now to questions
about Sappho and sexuality.

# 4. Sexuality and Ritual

THE OTHER PREOCCUPATION in the legends of antiquity has never ceased to exercise Sappho's readers: her sexuality. Among classical scholars it continues to arouse controversy, and it remains crucial for many other readers of her poetry. In the case of scholars interpreting her poetry, there is good reason to question the emphasis it has been given. Why read the works of a female poet primarily as the key to her emotional and sexual life, when those of her male contemporaries are examined for more impersonal, literary qualities? Sappho is not the only woman to receive more than her fair share of this kind of attention, and it is legitimate to query such an approach to women writers in general.

But there are some reasons why this is a legitimate question to ask about Sappho. Her poetry is one of the few sources of information that exist about love between women in the ancient world, and she has become a figurehead for many lesbian women. So it seems important to begin by addressing directly the question of whether she was lesbian, and to anticipate the conclusion of this chapter by saying that, on the whole, the best answer is yes. Sappho's poetry speaks clearly, to my mind, of an eroticism directed toward other women, even though it also includes some poems less easy to reconcile with modern ideas of a lesbian identity.

Yet the very fascination of this question for generations of readers means that it is full of pitfalls. Direct discussions of Sappho's sexuality come from a period much later than her own, and are filtered through the attitudes and assumptions of a culture already very different from hers. This kind of problem does not arise only in antiquity. Nineteenth-century scholars had their own version of the "two Sapphos" theory, with one school seizing disapprovingly on assertions about her love of women and the other leaping chivalrously to her defense: it became difficult for anyone mentioning the subject to avoid alignment on one side or the other. Similar attitudes continued into this century. One of the most amusing is that of the American critic David Robinson, who in a book published in 1924 devotes several pages to impassioned declamation about Sappho's "moral purity." Among the evidence he cites are her poetic skill and love of flowers: it is, he asserts, "against the nature of things" that these qualities should be found in "a child of sodden vice" (*Sappho and Her Influence*, 43–45). Scholarly antipathy to the idea that Sappho could have been lesbian has abated somewhat in more recent studies, but problems remain. Considerable interest has, for example, focused on a scrap of papyrus (99) that may or may not be by Sappho, on which one badly damaged word can be construed to read "receivers of the dildo." The attention lavished on this single word, in a fragmentary text of uncertain authorship, could be said to arise from the same kind of attitude to lesbian sexuality as the mime of Herodas discussed in the first chapter.

These prejudices are one hurdle, but there are even more difficult cultural gaps facing us. One of the major problems arises from the way in which sexual behavior is now categorized. Some of Sappho's poetry seems to express passionate love for women, but it also includes some traditional celebrations of marriage. Should we then conclude that she was bisexual? Questions asked in the late twentieth century about Sappho's sexuality reflect a whole set of prior assumptions, many of which may turn out to be inappropriate for her time and situation. So I begin by looking more closely at those assumptions and testing

*Sexuality and Ritual*

them against what is known of ancient society. Only after doing this, and reviewing the extremely scanty evidence about lesbianism in archaic Greece, will it be possible to turn back to what remains the most significant source, her poetry.

## Sexual Roles

To begin with definitions, including the terms I have already used: lesbian and bisexual. One definition of lesbianism is formulated by the author of a major study of ancient Greek homosexuality. In a brief discussion of lesbianism, K. J. Dover alludes to the question of whether Sappho and her companions "sought to induce orgasms in one another by bodily contact" (*Greek Homosexuality*, 182). But not everyone would agree that this is the most important question. The poet Adrienne Rich argues for a focus on emotional bonding between women in a patriarchal society, which may or may not include physical contact. Do questions about Sappho, then, presuppose this kind of strict and, some would say, reductive definition, or are we talking more generally about desire?

Then there are deeper questions about how people and behavior have been categorized along sexual and gender lines. If one looks at periods and cultures other than modern western societies, it soon becomes clear that to classify people and behavior as homosexual and heterosexual (with bisexual as an intermediate category) is not the only possibility. Sexual activity has often been characterized not according to the gender of the beloved but in terms of the role played by the lover. In ancient Greece and Rome and in many other societies too, including early modern Japan and Renaissance Europe, the most significant division is between active and passive roles in a homosexual relationship; and both partners would probably also relate to the opposite sex at some stage of their lives. This does not mean, though, that it would have made sense to their contemporaries to characterize them as bisexual: the division between the roles of lover and beloved was far more significant.

Another basis for drawing distinctions has been the extent of conformity with accepted gender roles. We have seen how gender is bound up with social and political structures: the main reason why tribadism was thought deviant was that it apparently involved someone from an inferior group taking on masculine power and privilege. Here too there are parallels for this phallocentric assumption that male sexual activity is the model for everyone, including lesbian women. Judith Brown, charting attitudes toward lesbianism in the medieval and early modern periods, suggests that the relative shortage of references to it can be attributed partly to an unquestioned assumption of male superiority. But this time the conclusion drawn was different from that of the Romans: lesbianism was viewed more indulgently than male homosexuality, on the grounds that the inferior sex was merely showing an understandable desire to emulate the superior one.

The importance of social roles in these accounts is a pointer to a basic difference between ancient ways of thinking about sexuality and those now current. The division of not only acts but also people into categories—homosexual, heterosexual, bisexual, lesbian—on the basis of their choice of sexual partner goes with an assumption that sexuality expresses something fundamental about a person's identity, revealing some kind of inner truth about her or him. But a growing body of historical work, much of it inspired by Michel Foucault, shows that it was only in the fairly recent past that we began to live our sexuality in this way. For the Greek world, much of the available evidence suggests the opposite: that sexual behavior, for a man at least, was regarded not as an expression of his innermost self, but as an index to his role and capacities in public life.

One of the clearest indications of this gap between ancient and modern assumptions is the way in which the Greeks and Romans viewed dreams. Today we are all to some extent Freudians, finding particular significance in dreams and especially in their hidden sexual content. For ancient interpreters, however, Freud's priorities are often reversed. One of the richest sources of ancient dream analysis is the work of a Greek writer from the Roman period, Artemidorus, who in the second century practiced dream interpretation as a profession. Many of the dreams he studied had an explicit sexual content, but his interpretations do not lead him into the depths of the dreamer's psyche. Sometimes, according to Artemidorus, sexual dreams hardly need interpreting: they simply represent in sleep the interests and desires of the dreamer when awake. But when he does offer to explain their significance, it is often to predict some future event in the dreamer's life or to indicate something about his standing or fortunes in the world. A man's dream about penetrating his brother, for example, is good because it indicates that "he will be above his brother and look down on him"; to have sex with one's grown son in a dream bodes well for a man who is away from home because it refers to their being together after his safe return (1.78). Men's dreams about penetrating their mothers, though quite widespread and varied in detail, are also interpreted symbolically. We are told, for example, that they are especially appropriate for leaders because "a mother signifies one's native country" (1.79), so that domination of her body indicates control of civic affairs. Nor is this way of thinking peculiar to a professional like Artemidorus. The history of Herodotus, writing seven centuries earlier, recounts how Hippias, the deposed tyrant of Athens, dreamed he was sleeping with his mother (6.107): he took it to mean that he would regain control of the city.

The connections drawn in these interpretations among sexual, social, and political roles are also found throughout the sources discussed by Foucault and by a growing number of classicists. There are now several studies based on classical Athens (the earliest period covered by Foucault, though still over a century later than Sappho). Focusing mainly on prose texts—rhetorical, medical, and philosophical—and concentrating as their sources do on male homosexuality, they show that the code governing a lover's conduct toward his beloved is closely linked to contemporary ideals about a good citizen's behavior. For the senior partner it is important to assume an active, dominant role in sexual relations just as he does in social life as a member of the elite body of male citizens. So closely are these two roles linked, in fact, that a grown man who adopts the alternative sexual role—a passive one—is stigmatized as unfit to exercise the rights of a citizen. For the younger partner, too, submitting to this role by accepting his lover's advances is potentially problematic, since it comes dangerously close to acting like a woman or a slave, which would be unworthy of the full-fledged citizen he is shortly to become. So there is also a well-defined set of rules for him, laying down the conditions under which he may gratify an older lover's desire for him. One of the most important is that he must not himself enjoy the sex or feel desire, as a woman would. His motives for accepting a lover should instead have to do with forming useful social and political connections; otherwise he will be derided as a prostitute.

For both lover and beloved, therefore, what is paramount is the adoption of an active, controlling role in relation both to others and to one's own desires. The same structure can be seen operating, according to these rules, at three different levels. In sexual relations the ideal citizen will be in a superior position both in relation to the boy he loves and in the control of his own desires. Self-control is even more crucial for the beloved boy, who will otherwise compromise his masculinity by welcoming the role of love object. Within the city all male citizens belong to a social group that will be dominant over others; and their city as a whole will have the upper hand over outsiders, especially non-Greeks (otherwise known as barbarians). What informs the prescription of these roles is not a concern that a man should be able to express his individuality, but rather that he maintain in his sexual life the kind of control essential to his social position: if he fails in the first sphere, he is disqualified in the second.

The recent spate of studies drawing attention to these structures has in many ways revolutionized the understanding of sexuality in the ancient world. Most obviously, they highlight the extent to which sexual roles, and the concept of sexuality itself, are socially constructed rather than naturally given. Second, and equally important, they show that for the ancient world we need to discard the idea of sexuality as the identity or attribute of an individual, and think instead in terms of types of behavior or ways of relating. Greek society, for these purposes, must be broken down not into a collection of individuals so much as into sets of roles and relationships, several of which may be adopted by one individual, whether all together or at different stages of life. The mature male citizens we have just been considering almost certainly had sexual relations with women as well as boys; what mattered was their masculine role, not their choice of object. The boys, though, probably confined their sexual relationships for the time being to their own sex: homosexuality in this sense tends, in ancient Greece, to be linked with the period of transition from childhood to adulthood, after which many men would, at least in terms of sexual acts, become bisexual.

I shall return later to the question of puberty, homosexuality, and sexual initiation. For the moment, the point to note in connection with Sappho is that Greek women are no more likely than men to have related exclusively to their own sex. This does not mean that individual inclination was entirely irrelevant. Many of the texts in which sexual behavior is discussed do, it is true, give the impression that men's passionate energies were directed overwhelmingly toward members of their own sex, not toward women. But they are not unanimous on this matter, and there are also places in Greek culture where men's erotic interest in women is explored. A favorite subject for painting on vases was satyrs, half-human, half-animal creatures who represent a fantasy of male excess: their main interests are drink and sex, and they are often shown in hot pursuit of women. Homosexual relationships between men, on the other hand, probably receive disproportionate attention in prose texts precisely because of the problems they pose for the younger partner. In Sappho's poetry the overwhelming impression is of an eroticism directed toward women, which may have involved individual choice as well as social convention. It is fairly certain, though, that she and most of her companions also engaged sexually with men at some point in their lives.

But there are many difficulties in relating these analyses of male homosexuality to Sappho and lesbianism, and indeed to female sexuality in general. There is the familiar source problem: the material on which they are based comes mainly from Athens and from a later period than Sappho's. They are about men, not women, and in detecting links between sexual and political roles they also show that we cannot extrapolate directly from men's homosexual roles to those of women, whose relation to the structures of power is a different one. Even more seriously, most ancient discussions set out not to describe sexual behavior, but to prescribe it. This point cannot be overstated: what we learn from most prose texts about male homosexuality is only the publicly accepted ideals of sexual etiquette within a small group of privileged men. The rhetorical texts in particular, some of them used in actual legal cases, are a prime example of special pleading which says more about the sticks available for beating one's opponent (often a political opponent) than about how people actually behaved.

These problems apply to all discussions of sexuality in the ancient world, but there is another specific to women. It will by now come as no surprise that almost all the information we have about women's sexuality was produced by men, in the context of a patriarchal society. One consequence is that direct discussions of lesbianism are almost nonexistent in archaic and classical sources. For once even classical Athens has almost nothing to offer, the only exception being two references in Plato to women who prefer their own sex (*Symposium* 191e; *Laws* 636ab).

For the archaic period the only available evidence, consisting of such things as vase paintings and poetry, is almost all indirect and very difficult to interpret. One possible allusion to lesbianism comes in a poem by the late sixth-century poet Anacreon about a girl the speaker desires: "but she—she comes from Lesbos with its fine cities—finds fault with my hair because it is white, and gapes after another" (358L). The fact that "another" is referred to by a feminine pronoun may indicate that the girl from Lesbos prefers women; but it has been argued that it could equally well refer to the poet's pubic hair and that she prefers fellatio, which according to Attic comedy was a speciality of women from Lesbos. Apart from this one controversial poem, by far the most substantial evidence is Sappho's poetry. Its importance is all the greater because, as well as being the clearest indication of sexual love between women, it is also one of the few moments in antiquity when we hear a woman's voice, unmediated by male authorship, expressing sexual desire.

Still that desire must be approached in a broader context: the ways in which sexuality, and women's sexuality in particular, figures in Greek culture. Although Sappho does not merely reproduce the dominant paradigms of her culture, neither does she write in complete isolation from them. Later we shall see how she negotiates with, often departs from, and sometimes subverts some of the patterns of erotic relationship found in the love poetry of her male contemporaries. But before this complex relationship can be understood, it needs to be situated within the social and symbolic practices of her time. The studies of male homosexuality give notice that sexual meanings may be found at unexpected points in ancient Greek culture: in particular, we need to be alert to the ways in which female sexuality is represented within shared, public meanings and practices. The fact that these are produced within a patriarchal culture then gives rise to questions about women's own experience: how did they relate to the stereotypes about them?

Again, the time and place for which the source material is richest is classical Athens, and so I shall continue to draw on material from there. But here too, political structures can be seen to determine much about the position of women, and we must bear in mind that women's sexuality was not interpreted in exactly the same way in democratic Athens and in the aristocratic milieu of Sappho's Lesbos.

## Female Sexuality and Patriarchal Ideology

It would be impossible to give a full account of how female
sexuality is represented in Greek culture and thought, since gendered categories appear in so many contexts, often unfamiliar
ones. Take the different ideas of justice in fifth-century Athenian
tragedies such as the *Oresteia* trilogy by Aeschylus or Sophocles'
*Antigone*. In both works archaic, family-based notions of justice
are associated particularly with women, in contrast to a newer,
more rationalized and more masculine kind of justice. The resulting battle of the sexes is significant thematically, not just for
the individuals involved. In both, women stand for something
beyond themselves, and what might in twentieth-century fiction
be facets of personality are instead emblematic of social and
symbolic forces at work in a whole society. Or take cosmology
and religion. The beginnings of the universe were in early Greece
cast in mythical terms, as the product of sexual encounters between gods, and human life too was felt to be determined by a
host of deities, all of whom were definitely gendered beings. One
of the most significant meanings of female sexuality for present
purposes has already been encountered in Artemidorus' dream
interpretations, and it is repeated in the Athenian betrothal formula: an Athenian father pledged his daughter in marriage to
her future husband with the words "I hand this woman over to
you for the plowing of legitimate children." This metaphorical
connection between women's bodies and the fruitful earth was
universal in the culture, and it is of crucial importance to the
religious roles allotted to females, both human and divine.

To turn for a moment to the opposite end of the scale: where
individual women were concerned, there was a fairly constant
set of stereotypes in circulation about their sexual behavior. For
many Greeks, including the Athenians, the single most obvious
fact about women and sex was their immoderate enjoyment of
it. According to myth, the prophet Teiresias owed his blindness
to having given the game away. He had lived both as a woman
and as a man, and was therefore well qualified to say which of

the sexes got more pleasure from intercourse. When asked, he said that the woman got nine-tenths of the pleasure and the man only one-tenth, whereupon the goddess Hera, furious at this betrayal of women's secrets, blinded him. Women were accordingly seen as creatures whose insatiable sexual desire had to be controlled by men.

The plays of Aristophanes present in comic form some male fantasies about what may happen if this control is relaxed. No fewer than three of his plays show women breaking out of their normal restraints and seizing power, in a way that is tolerable only because of the temporary license of a dramatic festival. In the process they reveal their (supposedly) true natures: in *Lysistrata* the women's sex strike all but crumbles because they themselves cannot endure the deprivation they are trying to inflict on men; and in *Women at the Thesmophoria* a group of participants in a women-only festival exchange notes about their deceptions of men, including frequent adultery.

Women's sexual energy was not always portrayed in a benign way. Linking women's bodies metaphorically with the earth suggests a positive valuation of their sexuality: human life depends on women's fruitfulness just as, in a largely agricultural economy, it depends on the earth's. But the fruitfulness is, especially in classical Greek thought, conditional on the proper cultivation of women through marriage. Women who are not yet married, or who have broken out of marital constraints, are linked through a darker set of images with the wild, uncivilized regions outside the polis, even with bestiality. It is normal to refer to an unmarried girl as *admētos*, which literally means untamed, and there is a plethora of uncomplimentary animal images for sexually active mature women, from the animal-wives in Semonides to the description of Clytaemnestra in Aeschylus' *Agamemnon* as a female monster, a Scylla or a snake. Suspicion of female sexuality is especially marked in democratic Athens and reflects a change in the function of marriage. As the formation of links between aristocratic dynasties became less important, the role of bride diminished, and a woman's role became limited to that of producing legitimate heirs. But since she came as an outsider to her husband's household, there would always be doubts about her loyalty, and hence about the legitimacy of her sons: so her sexuality had to be vigilantly watched.

The view of female sexuality as something in need of control also corresponds in interesting ways to the code for male sexuality. Whereas the ideal for Athenian males is that they should be able to moderate their sexual impulses, women are seen as sexually voracious and incapable of such control. The same relationship of negative to positive can also be seen by setting the assumed links between female nature and wildness alongside the idea of the city as a community of male citizens, a group of insiders who define themselves by contrast with noncitizen outsiders. Although women are in one sense, as those who produce citizens, central in the community, in another, with their wild and potentially uncivilized nature, they are outside it—and their uncontrolled sexuality helps to define what it is to be a citizen male just as the idea of nature defines that of civilization. From this perspective it looks as if these ideas about women and their sexuality are also a way of establishing masculine identity by representing what is not, or should not be, masculine. Women, together with slaves, animals, and barbarians, occupy the position of the other, the not-male-citizen, in a symbolic system that is, in Luce Irigaray's term, hommosexual: that is to say, essentially about men.

It is worth stressing again that this is far from being an objective or unmotivated description of what actually happened, or even of what was experienced as happening. If the accounts of the sexual attitudes appropriate to a male citizen represent an ideal that was not necessarily attained in everyday life, these ideas of women's sexual nature embody the mirror opposite, ratifying the social control of women by painting a vivid picture of the forces ranged on the other side. Hence in the few direct sources we have on women's behavior, including sexual behavior, the emphasis is on their subordination to their husbands. Prose writers like Xenophon and Aristotle prescribe control;

imaginative literature, in what is only an apparent contradiction, explores the consequences of slackening it.

But what about women's own experience of themselves as sexual beings? Inhabiting this patriarchal ideology would, one might think, present them with some problems. On one hand, women were supposed to occupy the position of the other, bearers of a potentially wild, unruly, uncivilized sexuality in opposition to which masculinity defined itself. Yet on the other, their fertility was a force that had to be both controlled and harnessed, in order to reproduce the community of male citizens. We may wish to ask how women lived this contradiction. Did they experience themselves as sexually voracious, or did they internalize the ethos of control prescribed for them? Or were there positions outside this opposition?

Like so many other areas of their lives, Greek women's sexual experience remains beyond our ken. But it is possible to go beyond seeing women's sexuality as a monolith and women as passive objects of description. In the first place, we can examine the sources in such a way as to reveal their biases and contradictions. Second, even from the limited and biased accounts of women available, it is possible to identify areas in which they participated actively in the symbolic practices of their culture, and to see that they could adopt a number of different attitudes toward official ideology. There is one area above all where women can be seen relating actively to the public meanings attached to their sexuality: religion.

Religious festivals were, especially in Athens, the most important occasions on which women played a role publicly recognized as vital to the whole community, and on which they could form, outside their homes, social links separate from those of men. These occasions give us a glimpse of groups of women acting independently, to some extent at least; and, most crucially, they can be seen as offering to the women who took part several different ways of engaging with the ideologies expressed in festivals, especially the more official ones. This is especially important because the rituals they performed were shot through with symbolism relating to human, agricultural, and divine fertility and sexuality.

Religious celebration normally involved the highly emotional experience of communal singing and dancing, recognized as hav- ing a socializing function. Rather than just reflecting the social roles prescribed for them, religious rituals will also have induced the desired behavior in the girls and women who enacted them. This means that the study of religion provides an angle on women's own experience of the constructions put upon their sexuality. It is also directly relevant to the study of Sappho, in whose poetry the worship of Aphrodite plays such an important part.

## Sexuality and Women's Festivals

I begin with the annual festival on which Aristophanes' play is based: the Thesmophoria, widely celebrated in the Greek world and one of the better-documented women's festivals. In Athens (though not always elsewhere) it took place in October-November, at the end of one season and shortly before the next crop was planted. Its patron goddess was Demeter, the goddess of corn and agriculture, and like many women's festivals it was concerned with fertility. It seems to have been an occasion involving citizen-wives in large numbers, and it took place at the heart of the city, near the symbolic centers of male political power. One source indicates that during the festival the normal business of political life was either suspended or conducted elsewhere. Involving three days of camping out in makeshift shelters, it was one of the few occasions on which women spent time away from their homes. Another feature marking its abnormality was that they temporarily organized themselves in structures modeled on the city's permanent institutions.

Despite the fact that the rituals were secret (and Aristophanes' play makes it clear how little he knows about them), some of what went on can be pieced together from scattered sources. On the first day the women went up the hill leading to the festival site, no doubt in a procession that involved some dancing. The second was a day of somber mood, when they devoted themselves to fasting and sexual abstinence, symbolized by their sitting on pallets made of plants thought to be antaphrodisiac. On the third, the day of Beautiful Birth, the fasting gave way to joyful feasting and celebration.

Other details of the rituals confirm that fertility was central, though the sequence of events is not exactly known. There was a ritual involving pits in the ground, into which pigs—symbolic of female genitals—and dough cakes shaped like phalluses had been thrown. During the festival a special category of women who had remained chaste for three days went down into the pits, brought up the rotting remains, and placed them on altars: it was thought that these remains, mixed with sown seed, would ensure a good harvest. Although interpreters of this festival are not agreed on all points, some features emerge that recur in other rites involving women. There is the by now familiar link between women's fertility and that of the earth. The secret recesses of the earth clearly have sexual connotations, and placing sexual objects in a pit reproduces the symbolic link made in the marriage formula between plowing and human intercourse. At the same time, the pattern of rotting followed by renewed growth repeats the cycle of annual death and rebirth in nature.

The link between women's and the earth's fertility, crucial to the ritual, is on one level cosmic and universal. But as enacted in this festival, it is closely tailored to the political and social structures of its time. To begin with, the participants are segregated into distinct groups. In this case participation is confined to women, but even in festivals open to both sexes the roles are usually distinct. The division involves not only gender but also, crucially, social status: here the participants are both married women and citizens, that is, women whose duty is to reproduce the city as an exclusive community. The importance of the Thesmophoria in particular is shown by one of the rules relating to it: husbands had to pay all the expenses when their wives attended the festival.

The social status of the women who participated, therefore,

meant that they were identified with the interests of the male elite who made up the polis, and this identification can also be traced in the symbolic practices of the festival. There are some interesting parallels with the idea of women's rampant sexuality and men's control. On one hand, the celebrants of the festival took on, for a few days, a masculine role. It is not just that, as citizen-wives, they were more closely linked than other women with the centers of power; they actually occupied the symbolic center of the city, displacing its normal business, and assumed some of its political structures. For the duration of the festival they elected magistrates (archons, or in the feminine, Thesmophorian version, archousai) from among their number and made decisions by majority vote. On the other hand, the symbolism of pigs and caverns, and the link with Demeter, marked their part as a feminine one. Yet this focus on female sexuality and fertility was at the same time contained by its opposite, the insistence on chastity during the festival and, for some, before it as well. In political terms, then, the Thesmophorians were representing themselves both as central to the city (by taking it over) and as marginal (because the takeover was temporary), while in sexual terms they celebrated both fertility and chastity. Since their sexuality was essential to the city's stability but could also disrupt it, the contradictions at these two levels are clearly linked. The Thesmophorian women enacted not one but both sides of the gender divide as represented in the city's ideology: although they reproduced the divide in their rituals, they were not confined to one or the other side of it. It is already clear that individuals could relate to the ideology of gender in complex ways.

Some of these themes can be traced in other women's festivals. At the Scira, a one-day Athenian festival probably confined to women, the participants are said to have eaten garlic to discourage sexual attention from men. At the Haloa, another festival linked with Demeter, they handled models of male and female genitals, some made of dough and placed on tables at the feast; they also spoke freely of sex in a way our Christian informant finds shameful, but which may just have involved fertility.

Though less is known about these festivals than about the

Thesmophoria, these details, gleaned from various sources, suggest that they probably reproduced the Thesmophorian focus, carefully controlled, on female fertility. They also share another feature, in giving rise to male fears about what a group of women, temporarily alone and powerful, might get up to. In another of Aristophanes' plays about insubordinate women, *Assemblywomen,* it is at the Scira that they meet and hatch their revolutionary plans. Outside comic contexts, these fears appear in more violent and disturbing form. Herodotus in the fifth century links the founding of the cult with the fifty daughters of Danaus, who on their wedding night in Egypt murdered their husbands (2.171); another, later story has the celebrants of the festival castrating a man who has spied on their rituals (Aelian 44).

Although the Thesmophoria is not represented in Sappho's poetry, it is a useful starting point for considering the links between religion and sexuality. In an area about which information is so thin, its practices are relatively well documented, and it shows how female sexuality could be represented at the most public, civic end of the spectrum of social practices. It also forms a striking contrast with a festival that does figure in Sappho, in which a rather different atmosphere seems to have prevailed: the Adonia, a more informal occasion that was not part of the official state calendar of events. It is thought to have taken place in July, at the height of summer, and like the Thesmophoria it deals with the processes of vegetation. For this festival, seeds were planted on pieces of terracotta and taken up to the flat rooftops of private houses. For a time they were watered, and the seeds sprouted; but then they were allowed to parch and die, and were thrown into the sea or a spring. At the same time, an image of Adonis was consigned to the water. The climax seems to have been a night of loud and unrestrained lament over Adonis.

Everything known of the Adonia suggests a festival quite different in spirit from those just considered. For one thing, the rules for participation were much less strict. A comedy from the fourth century BCE by Menander has women neighbors celebrating it in an informal group, concubines and citizen-wives together. There are also some indications in comedy that, although men did not participate in this festival, they were less rigorously excluded from it than from others: more than one male comic character complains that the festivities on the rooftops are too loud and riotous to be ignored. The young man who describes the party in Menander says it kept him awake (*The Girl from Samos*, 43–44), and a character in Aristophanes' *Lysistrata* complains that assembly proceedings have been interrupted by a woman wailing for Adonis from the rooftops (389–398).

The differences continue. The goddess of this festival is not Demeter but Aphrodite, whose sexual aspect, though linked with fertility, is not tied to it. And although the growth and withering of the "gardens of Adonis" probably alludes to fertility, this element is far less prominent. Descriptions of the festival suggest that the symbolism of human and agricultural fertility pervading the Demeter festivals was largely absent from the Adonia: instead, the most remarked-upon activity at this and other informally organized women's cults is noisy and enjoyable private merrymaking. At the other end of the spectrum from the Thesmophoria, then, we seem to glimpse a world in which the city's official writ did not run, in which women were released from the burden of being responsible for national fertility and simply got together, without a script, to have a good time.

Where does this leave Greek women in relation to the official view of their sexuality? It does look as if the festivals allowed for some complex relationships to the ideology that marked them so strongly as sexual beings. In some, female sexuality was linked with agricultural fertility, in others less so. Participants in the Thesmophoria acted out both sexual expression and its opposite; the Adonia apparently emphasized emotional release more than sexual symbolism. Even our limited knowledge is enough to show that different festivals provided women with different ways of enacting the construction of their own sexuality. The very fact that there was such variety between festivals, some open to limited groups of women, some to the same women at different times, some a matter of public duty and some of private enjoyment, suggests that there was a range of sexual stances for women, influenced but not entirely governed by their social status.

But one feature common to all these festivals emerges. They are viewed by the men who describe them with unease and sometimes fear, showing that the contradictions they embody are dynamic and must constantly be renegotiated. Women's sexuality is a powerful force, which festivals both harness and are always threatening to unleash on society. From a female perspective, however, this probably led to a sense of empowerment. Even if only for a short time, women were seen as a potentially powerful and independent group, and it is hard to imagine that they did not come away from such events with an enhanced sense of themselves and their sexual energies.

The most important point about women's festivals is that the meanings attached to female, as well as male, sexuality in ancient Greece can be found at the level of public as well as private life—and this can tell us something about women's own experience as well as about men's view of them. The powerful emotional and sexual expression at festivals may not always have taken place in a context as public as the Thesmophoria; but it was always communal and took women outside the confines of their domestic lives. Given that festival space and time were not just abnormal but supranormal, it is at least possible that it was here, rather than in individual relationships, that many Greek women experienced themselves most powerfully as sexual beings. In the twentieth century we tend to place more emphasis on the private, individual experience of sexual intercourse as a high point of emotional and physical fulfillment. It need not have been so in Greek culture. The stereotype certainly was that women enjoyed physical sex enormously, and medical texts (by men) report that they experienced orgasm. But there is no reason to think that this pleasure carried the same charge as it does in contemporary culture. On the contrary, it seems that in order to find in ancient Greek culture a sense of the significance of sexuality for women, we have to look at shared symbolism and experience, especially in religion. Certainly in reading Sappho's love poetry it is important to be aware of its communal significance, of its suprapersonal dimension as well as the personal experience that seems at first to be its subject.

## Sexuality and the Gods

Another way of appreciating the place of female sexuality in the public symbolism of Greek culture is by looking more closely at the gods. Greek religion was polytheistic: an enormous range of gods were worshipped at all levels of public and private life, from the patron deities of major cities such as Athena down to the deities of local cult and semidivine figures such as the Nereids. The group about which we know most is that represented in Homer as a kind of extended family, living on Olympus with Zeus at their head. Of the Olympians, four—Hera, Athena, Artemis, Aphrodite—are female. To these can be added a fifth, Demeter, patroness not only of the Thesmophoria but also of another important cult, the Eleusinian mysteries; she and Dionysus, though they barely figure in Homer, were increasingly recognized as equal in importance to the ten Homeric Olympians. The roles of these deities, and especially their sexual behavior, provide another angle on the significance attached to sexuality and gender. As with festivals, the gods represent many of the assumptions of the patriarchal society that imagined them. But again it will become clear that the ideology they embody is not monolithic: there is some room for maneuver, some space for choice between deities and different views of them.

Like most gods, the Greek deities were both like and unlike humans. They had in common with humans birth, but not death: they ate and drank, but ambrosia and nectar replaced the food and drink of humans. As gods they were capable of superhuman feats, but they did not observe superior standards of morality, even though to some extent they were guarantors of morality for humans. In fact, they appear somewhat amoral, especially in their sexual behavior. All the gods have a sexual aspect, which for male gods is expressed in relation not only to goddesses (usually lesser ones) but also to human females. Mythology is full of tales of the pursuit and rape of women by gods, an event that because of their divinity invariably leads to pregnancy. There is an obvious correlation between the role of divine pursuer and the role that contemporary culture assigned to upper-class males. These divine pursuits are with very few exceptions heterosexual, the best-known exception being the seizing of the youth Ganymede by Zeus. Here too, though, the division of roles into active and passive is reproduced, with the senior partner playing an unproblematically masculine role.

With goddesses the situation is more complicated, no doubt partly because of the difficulty of combining the power appropriate for deities with the idea of female sexuality as a wild force in need of control. Hence two of the goddesses are, unlike any of their male counterparts, virgins. Athena is a notoriously male-identified goddess who often appears dressed as a warrior and does not even have a mother: she sprang fully armed from the head of Zeus, who had swallowed her pregnant mother Metis. Artemis is a slightly more paradoxical figure: she acquired somewhere in her history the function of presiding over childbirth, so that her separation from sexuality is not as complete as Athena's. Her most familiar aspect, however, is as a virgin associated with hunting and wild animals. This makes her not so much an asexual goddess as one associated with the threshold of sexual life. Although both Artemis and Athena sometimes, like human maidens, arouse desire in others, neither is shown initiating sexual contact as all the male gods do. So far, then, there is a fairly clear double standard on Olympus, as on earth.

The sexual aspect of the remaining major goddesses always has some connection with fertility, but it takes very different forms. The connection is most obvious in the case of Demeter, the goddess of corn and agriculture, whose daughter Persephone was playing with a group of other young girls when she was seized and carried off by the god of the underworld, Hades (Pluto for the Romans). Demeter's grief and anger at her daughter's loss caused the earth to cease being fruitful, a crisis eventually resolved by an agreement that Persephone should spend part of the year on earth with her mother and part below with her husband. Her bond to the underworld and her initiation into sexual experience are symbolized by the fact that while below the earth she received from Hades the gift of a pomegranate and ate some of its seeds. The fullest version of this story is found in a seventh-century BCE hymn to Demeter written in the language and style of Homer, and in many of its details it functions as a kind of charter for the Thesmophoria.

The most striking feature of this myth is the way it reinforces the idea of female sexuality as a cosmic force by associating it with two goddesses and portraying it as a world-shattering power. Agricultural fertility, and potentially human life, is temporarily destroyed by Demeter's mourning, and Persephone's annual disappearance from and return to the earth is also linked with the cycle of vegetation. But the myth is equally interesting for the way in which it articulates and distributes different female roles and statuses. Persephone represents the pubescent girl, as indicated by her other common name Kore, another term for maiden. Like many girls in Greek literature on the threshold of marriage, she is first shown in carefree play with her friends, picking flowers in a "soft meadow" (*Homeric Hymn to Demeter 7*).

Hades snatches her away from this idyllic scene to be his bride, and here too there are clear parallels with contemporary social practice. She herself plays a passive part: Hades seizes her with the complicity of her father Zeus, while her mother's wishes play no part in the initial agreement and are only partially accommodated after a period of crisis. Finally there is the position of mother, occupied by Demeter herself. Of the three roles of maiden, wife, and mother, Persephone occupies the first two by turns. Demeter, though, is associated only with the third: in the hymn she is portrayed as a mother only, though there is passing mention of her sexual liaisons in other sources. So although the hymn celebrates her as maternal and fertile, it does not show her as a sexual being in relation to her peers. Persephone, on the other hand, though shown as a bride, is the object of rape by a male deity rather than a sexual subject.

Some of the spheres of sexual activity divided between Demeter and her daughter are brought together in Hera and Aphrodite, but to different effect in each case. In Hera's case, the earth's fertility is directly associated with sexual intercourse through the story of her union with Zeus, who is both her brother and her husband. In book 14 of the *Iliad*, wishing to distract Zeus from what is going on in the fighting between Greeks and Trojans, Hera seduces him. As they are about to lie down together on Mount Ida

> under them earth flowered delicate grass
> and clover wet with dew; then crocuses
> and solid beds of tender hyacinth
> came crowding upwards from the ground
> (*Iliad* 14.347–349, tr. Fitzgerald)

This archetypal scene of marital sex is repeated in visual renderings found in Hera's sanctuaries and accords with her principal role in cult, that of patroness of weddings; a secondary sphere of influence is maidenhood, the condition that immediately precedes marriage. The *Iliad*'s portrait of Hera as a wife, though, is remarkably negative: she is quarrelsome, jealous of Zeus's many amours, and murderous toward them and their offspring. This negativity is not redeemed by any positive relationship to either motherhood or sexuality. As consort to Zeus, she is faithful but mutinous; though a mother, she is never shown cherishing her children, and indeed can express considerable hostility toward them, as in the case of Hephaestus, who was so misshapen at birth that she hurled him into the sea. Though Hera does, then, combine elements of all the roles articulated in the myth of Demeter and Persephone, it is a combination full of conflict. And though all these goddesses represent sexuality as a cosmic force, there is not one in whom it is as unproblematically active as it is for the male gods.

So far we have a group of goddesses in whom several stages of women's lives, all defined in relation to their sexuality, are kept separate: those of maiden (Artemis, Persephone), bride (Persephone), mature wife (Hera), and mother (Demeter). Athena is if anything a parthenos, but she is a special case because of her asexuality and masculine qualities. All these goddesses are in turn differentiated from gods by the fact that none of them engages in active erotic pursuit, whether of divinities or mortals. The only possible exception to this is Hera's seduction of Zeus, but unlike the gods' exploits this takes place within marriage.

Against this background Aphrodite, the goddess of sexuality itself and one of the most ancient and powerful of deities, emerges as a remarkable figure. She shares other goddesses' association with fertility: in Hesiod's *Theogony*, when she first steps on the island of Cyprus after her birth, vegetation springs up magically beneath her feet as it did for Zeus and Hera. But her generative power goes even further. Hesiod, writing in the seventh century BCE, dates her birth from the mythical separation of earth and sky, and the philosopher Empedocles in the fifth names her as the principle whereby the four elements combine to form the world. For both she represents a fundamental cosmic principle of combination.

Thus it is not surprising that in her person and powers she breaches many of the boundaries just noted. As goddess of sexual attraction, she is concerned with erotic relationships of all kinds, both within and outside marriage, heterosexual and homosexual. There are hints of bisexuality both in her birth (she was born from the severed genitals of Uranus, the sky) and in her cult: a seventh-century image seems to show her with a beard. In myth she is not confined to one sexual relationship: although married to Hephaestus, she has sexual liaisons with other males, including not only deities, such as Ares (with whom she is caught by her husband in the *Iliad*), but also mortals. She has a son, Aeneas, for whom she cares and whom she is shown rather ineffectually helping in the *Iliad*: so although her maternal aspect is not strongly marked, it still contributes to a combination of roles not found in any other major goddess. Finally, and most strikingly, she is the pursuer of her mortal lovers, taking a role that among the Olympians is otherwise reserved for male gods. In one of the Homeric hymns about her, she is shown falling in love with the mortal Anchises and approaching him as he tends his cattle; and we have already encountered some of the other young men she loved, Adonis and Phaon. A primeval, cosmic, female deity whose power no one, not even Zeus, can resist and who shows an alarming propensity to transgress boundaries—it is not surprising that, while Aphrodite is celebrated in literature, she is also often regarded with fear and suspicion. In Homer she can be fearsome as well as charming, and in fifth-century Athenian tragedy her power is often destructive, as in Euripides' *Hippolytus*, where in a terrible act of revenge she brings about the death of a young man who honored the virginal Artemis above her. This makes it all the more remarkable that she appears far more often in Sappho's poetry than any other deity, and that she is shown in a wholly favorable light.

It must be pointed out that this simplified sketch of the goddesses somewhat exaggerates the differences between them. Looking more fully at their role in cult practice as against myth would bring out many similarities: they can all, for example, be honored by groups of young girls who are dedicated to them for a fixed period, and they all delight in singing and dancing and in female beauty and charm. Their association with this crucial stage of female life shows that they are not just archetypal figures: all of them, not only Aphrodite, are associated with moments of transition and hence by definition with what escapes the limits of particular roles and statuses.

But this schematic and artificially synchronic view of the major goddesses does highlight some correspondences between their roles and those prescribed for real women. Like human females, they tend to be linked with agricultural fertility and to be differentiated in terms of their sexual status. But apart from Aphrodite, they do not normally combine the roles of fully sexual female and mother; nor do they take an active role in sexual relations. This separation of roles reflects the need of a patrilineal society to limit the sexual activity of those women required to produce legitimate sons, and the gaps in it confirm that it represents a slanted perspective. There are, for example, few divine mother-daughter relationships represented in mythology but many mother-son ones, and no hint of lesbianism even in Aphrodite. Finally, it is telling that the deity who represents sexuality most fully is female, and often portrayed as untrustworthy, whereas Athena, particular friend of the hero Odysseus and patron deity of Athens, is the least sexual of the goddesses.

Still, if the goddesses can be seen as articulating female sexuality within a patriarchal system, it is also clear that there is room for a range of perspectives on the ideology they represent. They patronize different festivals: it is not surprising that the Demeter and Persephone myth, with its stress on fertility but careful insulation of motherhood from mature sexuality, should be linked with two major Athenian state festivals, the Thesmophoria and the Eleusinian mysteries. But the Adonia, which is quite different, must have been open to some of the same women; and its reputation for encouraging female license becomes easier to understand in view of the part played in it by Aphrodite, the mature and active lover of a beautiful young man. And outside the Olympic pantheon there is a whole assortment of minor and local deities, many with a sexual aspect: women's choice among them may have been partly a matter of tradition and locality, but there was surely some room for preference too.

To summarize, then. We have seen some of the ways in which female sexuality figures within a public set of meanings: the religious practices and symbols of Greek society. In this very selective sampling of women's festivals and female deities, my aim has been to provide a background for understanding the religious aspect and symbolism of Sappho's poetry. Within a clearly patriarchal symbolic framework, we have again found a clear tendency to associate women strongly with sexuality and fertility. The link with fertility can be both welcomed and feared, depending on the part women play in social and political structures; but there is a widespread taboo on active sexual expression by women, except in special contexts, and a pattern in the major female goddesses of separating the roles of maiden, wife, and mother. This set of archetypes is not, however, a stable, monolithic system: it can be contested from positions both within and outside it. The possibilities for challenge can be encapsulated in the boundary-breaching figure of Aphrodite.

At this point we can begin narrowing the focus onto Sappho and her world—but again the shortage of sources about women means that it will have to be done by a detour through the world of men. Bearing in mind the religious and social context already outlined, I shall approach the eroticism of Sappho's poetry indirectly, looking first at the construction of sexuality within the symposium, the main forum for erotic poetry by men.

## Sex and the Symposium

Earlier I outlined in general terms the social and political importance of the symposium. It has two more specific aspects that are important here. First, like girls' choruses, it had an educational function. Symposia were essentially an all-male affair: the only women admitted, as attendants or entertainers, were slaves. Also present, though, were boys and youths who had not yet attained adult status but would eventually become full members of the group (fig. 10). They were differentiated from the men by being allowed only to sit rather than recline; or they might act as wine pourers, as we are told Sappho's brother Larichus did (203). For them, attending symposia seems to have been part of their induction into full manhood and the social standing that went with it, and their presence helps to explain the existence of a body of poetry addressed specifically to boys and offering advice on subjects like friendship and wealth.

But there were many other songs performed on these occa- sions which show a side of the symposium very different from the sober one presented by Xenophanes. This was also an occasion for fantasizing about, and no doubt pursuing, sexual pleasure, whether with other male symposiasts or with the female slaves. The scenes of orgiastic revelry shown on many vases from the mid sixth century on may not match the reality exactly. But they do suggest that these occasions, as well as idealizing aristocratic behavior, also gave men the opportunity to relax normal restraints.

Yet the social relations of the symposium also structure the eroticism of both vase paintings and love poetry. Most obviously, the relationships painted and sung about are generally, like those in the classical period, between unequal partners. In the case of males, the usual relationship is between a man and a youth. This can go hand in hand with the symposium's educational function: the boy's lover is also his mentor, and in fact the advice poetry mentioned earlier, by Theognis, is addressed to a youth whose lover he is. Sexual relations with slave women have, on the other hand, no such elevated aims, and here the disparity in status is very sharp indeed.

The sexual relationships represented in this specialized context are clearly not the only ones that took place: future citizens, essential to the aristocratic community's survival, could not be born of pederastic relationships or from liaisons with slave women. So the erotic patterns of sympotic love poetry do not fully represent the sexual behavior either of the symposiasts or of the larger society. This is a mediated view that bears the marks of, once again, the symposiasts' need to assert their dominance over the outside world. The pattern of inequality and dominance in erotic relations can be seen particularly well in the love poetry of Anacreon, who wrote later than Sappho but whose erotic poetry has survived in greater quantities than that of closer contemporaries such as Alcaeus.

Some of Anacreon's poems suggest fairly equal relationships, even between men and youths. In others, especially the more obviously fictional ones, there are two distinct patterns, both asymmetrical. The singer tells of his relationship either with a younger beloved, whether boy or girl, or with Eros, the young god whose name in Greek means "desire." Eros is often associated with Aphrodite and sometimes represented as her son, though at times he is little more than a personification of the power of desire. In Anacreon he appears as an adversary who is always subduing the speaker or trying to, and a series of striking images describes this role. In one fragment Eros is a blacksmith who "once more took his great hammer and / struck, then dunked me in the icy stream" (413). Elsewhere he is a formidable opponent with whom the speaker boxes or whose bonds he is trying to escape.

Sometimes, though, the relationship described is not with Love himself but with the object of the speaker's passion. What is striking here is the tendency for the same adversarial relationship to be reproduced, but this time with the speaker in the dominant role. A good example is a well-known poem addressed to a sexually inexperienced girl in which, by a common erotic metaphor, she is compared to an untamed foal that the speaker imagines himself bridling and riding:

> I tell you: I'd soon bridle you,
> then take the reins and swing you
> round the far end of the track
>   (417)

The same scenario of erotic domination is clearly present in several poems addressed to boys.

Both kinds of relationship are structured in the same way, despite the reversal of roles in the second group: they are different sides of the same coin. And it seems far from accidental that, when the other figure in the poem is a human love object, it is the speaker who takes the dominant role. This is linked with the status of those who attended symposia. It would be unacceptable for the aristocratic symposiast to represent himself as unmanned by love for the figures in the poems, who are his juniors and thus his social inferiors. The figure of Eros, a god, is used to represent love as shattering and disorientating, but where other humans are concerned the speaker is the one in control, repeating his endless gesture of erotic mastery over those outside the charmed circle of his fellow drinkers. Love poetry, then, is no less structured by the social and political nature of the symposium than battle songs or poems about enemies.

It is important to bear this link in mind if we are trying to read Sappho's sexuality from her poetry, because it is a reminder that archaic love poetry is not directly descriptive or autobiographical. Rather, it promotes certain patterns of relationship whose importance is as much social as individual. It has some of the same normative aspects as the prose sources studied by Foucault—and where male lovers are concerned, it promotes similar patterns of inequality. In order to be alert to these aspects of Sappho's love poetry, we must return to the question of her audience. Girls and women could not occupy the same privileged social position as Alcaeus' and Anacreon's companion drinkers, and we can expect this difference to be represented in the poetry sung by and for them.

The symposium is a well-documented institution, and it is not difficult to find material illustrating the link between its social function and the ways in which it constructed male sexuality. Information about women's social groupings is far more sketchy. But the arguments I have outlined about the groups for which Sappho wrote some of her poetry point to a role for sexuality that is equally central, if not more so.

## Sex and Girls' Choruses

The status of parthenos is linked with sexuality in two ways. It is defined in terms of sexual relations, denoting the stage of life preceding marriage; and it has erotic connotations. To approach

marriage is by definition, in this perfect world, to become sexually attractive, and this desirable quality in maidens is indicated
in a number of ways. The mythical settings in which groups of
parthenoi are shown are full of sexual symbolism. Nausicaa in
book 6 of the *Odyssey* is playing ball (99–101), a motif that
recurs in erotic contexts elsewhere; in the *Homeric Hymn to
Demeter* Persephone is in a meadow, picking flowers (6–10). Not
only is this activity particularly appropriate, as a commentator
on Sappho tells us, for those who consider themselves "beautiful
and ripe" (122), but the individual flowers—roses, crocuses,
hyacinths, narcissi—all have erotic associations.

A particularly important context in which eroticism figures is
the poems written by Alcman for maiden choruses. An opening
invocation to Calliope calls upon her to invest all aspects of the
choir's performance with erotic allure:

> Come Muse, Calliope daughter of Zeus,
> begin the lovely verses: set
> desire on the song, and make the dancing graceful.
> (27)

And in two fairly lengthy, though still fragmentary, poems, the
chorus sing the praises of individual chorus members, indicating
that their appearance and grooming also contributed to the desire they aroused.

The ways in which these nubile parthenoi are celebrated recall
erotic descriptions elsewhere, including some in Sappho. In fragment 1, although the exact situation is unclear, the chorus mention the luxurious ornaments with which, like the members of
Euripides' chorus, individuals vie for favor: gold jewelry and, as
in Sappho's poem about adornment (98), clothes dyed in costly
purple and Lydian headgear, "the glory of dark-eyed girls"
(1.68–69). Particularly prominent are two leaders of the dance,
whose beauty is praised in a series of comparisons indicating
their high status: Agido resembles the sun or a noble horse
who stands out among grazing herds (41, 45–49), while

Hagesichora's hair, yellow like that mentioned in Sappho's poem, "blooms like pure gold" (51–54).

In a shorter but less enigmatic fragment, the chorus praise a young woman named Astymeloisa:

> holding a garland,
> like a bright star
> shining through the heavens
> or a golden shoot, or soft down
> . . . she passed through on slender feet
> and . . . the moist grace of [perfume]
> sat on [her] maidenly hair.
> (3.65–72)

Again many elements of this description are traditional, and several recur in Sappho: the garlands, the comparison with a bright heavenly body, the image of softness, the perfume, the focus on Astymeloisa's hair (or, according to another reading, on the chorus' own hair). Her companions also make explicit the effect her charms have on them, when they sing

> with limb-loosening desire, more meltingly than love
> and death she regards [me]
> (3.61–62)

and later, in a badly damaged line, ask "whether perhaps she might love me" and hope that "she might take my soft hand" (79–80).

In another context, such lines might easily be mistaken for confessions of private passion. But not only is the scenario a highly public one—Astymeloisa is described as passing "through the crowd, the darling of the people"—it is also likely that the singers give voice to their desire as a group, using the conventional choral I even though singing together. The love they express for Astymeloisa, far from being unique to any one of them, is a mark of her desirability, and hence her readiness for the destiny that awaits them all: marriage. The erotic verse that later tradition credited to Alcman thus includes some in which it is the female chorus members, not the poet himself, who sing of their desire; and, in keeping with the purpose and nature of choral song by maidens, the focus is on the girl capable of arousing such desire. Eroticism in girls' choruses is, then, just as closely tied to a socially defined role as that expressed by male symposiasts.

But to say that eroticism was institutionalized in girls' choirs is not to divorce it from lived experience. For symposia there is a wealth of evidence, particularly in vase paintings, to suggest that there was some correspondence between the sentiments expressed in love poetry and sexual practices, including homosexual intercourse. But whereas myriad vases show lovemaking between men, or between men and women, there are almost no unambiguous representations of women or girls making love. This does not of course mean that it never happened: women's invisibility here simply reflects, as usual, their invisibility in the public, male-dominated world. On the contrary, the fact that men did not stop at merely singing about love strongly suggests that girls did not either.

In the case of Spartan girls' choruses, the parallel with boys has provided another basis for thinking that homosexual lovemaking was a part of their initiation into adulthood. Both in Sparta and elsewhere in the Greek world, it seems that boys regularly spent time segregated from the rest of society, engaged in activities designed to train them in citizenship and manliness; and these activities, we are told, included pederastic relationships. In Crete we hear of ritual abductions of boys by older lovers, who would spend a fixed period of two months with them in the forest. Then the boys returned with their lovers to the city for ceremonies marking their new adult status, and each would be given armor and a drinking cup by his lover to symbolize his entry into the adult male community. Later Plutarch tells of a similar structure in the famous Spartan system of education, with boys acquiring at the age of twelve an older lover chosen from among the city's elite young men. There are clear parallels with the homosexual liaisons evoked in sympotic love poetry: these too are asymmetrical relationships, between a younger and an older partner, in which sexuality and education are in some way combined. This time, though, it is clear that they are not individual, chosen relationships, but institutionalized ones involving sharply defined age groups. Since the other activities of such groups will also have included choral dancing and dedication to a god, the parallels with girls' choirs are even closer than in the case of symposia.

There is, indeed, one clear piece of direct evidence about this connection. Plutarch's long discussion of education and pederasty includes a typically brief mention of women. Educational pederasty was, he says, so favored in archaic Sparta that "aristocratic women also became the lovers of young girls" (*Life of Lycurgus* 18). This statement, together with the parallels already mentioned, has led some scholars to argue that the choruses for which Alcman wrote reproduced all the structural features of boys' education. According to this view, not only did girls' choruses include eroticism as part of the participants' education for womanhood, but they also involved hierarchically structured sexual relationships between girls and women.

Plutarch's casual halfsentence does reinforce the natural supposition that this transitional time for girls involved homosexual experience, as it certainly did for boys. On one detail, though, he may be less than trustworthy: the asymmetrical structure of these relationships. The sexual ideal expressed in symposia is clearly tied to power: the lover represents himself as socially superior to his beloved. The initiatory relationships between young men and boys in Crete and Sparta are also unequal: it is as if entry to the elite takes place through a temporary and ritualized assumption of the inferior role. But it is unlikely that similar patterns governed erotic relationships between women, who could never assume that kind of power in society. Plutarch's aside hardly suggests a pressing interest: though he has broken the usual silence about women's relationships, he (or his source, since he was writing many centuries later) has probably assumed without further thought that they mimicked men's.

There is (apart from Sappho's poetry) some support in visual sources for the suggestion that the model for love between women was not a strictly hierarchical one, though the evidence is difficult to interpret. The most unambiguous image, and that closest to Sappho in time, is a painting on a late seventh-century BCE plate from Thera (now Santorini), a Spartan colony (fig. 11). It shows two women face to face; each holds a garland in one hand and touches her companion with the other. This is an erotic scene: garlands and the gesture of touching the chin are both found repeatedly in scenes of homosexual love between men. For some time this scene has been regarded as the only visual image of female homoeroticism from the archaic period. A recent study, however, suggests that scenes of women sharing a single cloak, repeated on black-figure vases, may also represent erotic relations (fig. 12). On a pot now at the University of Mississippi, two women sharing a cloak appear side by side with two love-making scenes, one heterosexual and one with two male figures, and the connection seems pretty clear.

All these scenes show, at first glance, a striking difference from corresponding representations of men. Two male lovers are almost always differentiated by age: an older bearded man woos a beardless youth (fig. 13). In the scenes showing women, there are no such obvious differences: the two figures are roughly equal. Still, the situation is complicated by the fact that there are no established conventions for indicating age differences between women, and it can be argued that both the Thera plate and some of the shared-cloak scenes do reveal slight differences of emphasis. On the Thera plate, although the two figures are roughly the same height, the one on the left is slightly more substantial and her chin-touching gesture suggests that she is taking the lead; the figure on the right is slimmer and apparently less dominant, and she probably held a flower in her hand, symbolizing attractiveness. Some of the cloak scenes seem to show one figure as slightly larger than the other; in others no difference can be discerned.

But the very absence of clear-cut distinctions for women shows that they are less significant in the culture than those between men. So the slight differences between some of these female figures may be accidental; or they may be dictated by the composition; or they may be influenced by the iconography of male homoeroticism. It seems clear, at all events, that while asymmetry is strongly marked when erotic relations between men are portrayed, in the case of female figures either there is no asymmetry or it is relatively insignificant.

## Sexuality and Sappho's Poetry

It should be apparent by now that the sexual element of Sappho's poems has many aspects that cannot be reduced to a single question about her own sexuality or that of her companions. The poems for which she has become best known, where one female voice expresses desire for another, represent only one facet of an eroticism that suffuses her poetry, and whose other elements include traditional symbols such as flowers, garlands, and singing itself, the celebration of marriage, and the worship of appropriate deities.

We have seen that this eroticism is conditioned in many ways by the culture of Sappho's time. The cultivation of beauty in aristocratic women, especially in parthenoi, is inseparable from their primary social function. Even apparently personal expressions of desire can, in some contexts, function as conventional praise of a girl who is readying herself for marriage, as Alcman's maiden songs show. And in singing such praises the young chorus members, like those who sang Sappho's wedding songs, are themselves being initiated into their role as desirable brides. There is even the possibility, suggested by parallels with the initiation of boys elsewhere, that lovemaking itself was part of a socializing process for girls at this transitional stage of life.

To this educational aspect of eroticism we can add its political and religious dimensions. Alliances formed through marriage were often politically important, and the vocabulary of female love and friendship in Sappho may well have had specific political resonances: women and girls from families in alliance might lavish praise on each other's charms, and withhold it from members of rival families. But love is also a cosmic power, embodied in supernatural beings and celebrated in communal acts of worship; here too the collective and the personal cannot be separated. Yet the parallels that enable us to explore the wider significance of sexual expression in Sappho do not account for every element of her work. In two of the areas discussed earlier, her poetry emerges as distinctive.

126

## FESTIVALS AND DEITIES

The deities who figure in Sappho's poems include the Muses, the Graces, and Hera, who shared a sanctuary on Lesbos with Zeus and Dionysus. By far the most prominent deity, though, is Aphrodite, who appears more often than any other god, even Eros. She haunts Sappho's poems in many guises. Several songs present poet and goddess in dialogue, and Sappho frequently calls on Aphrodite for assistance. But she is not the only one to feel the goddess' power. Other worshippers summon her to the sacred shrine in which they are gathered (2) or send offerings of rich perfumed cloth (101). She is responsible for both beauty and its effects on others. In attendance at weddings (194), she sheds beauty and erotic allure over the bride (112), and she is present in a young girl's first passion:

> Truly, sweet mother, I cannot do my weaving:
> I am overcome with desire for a boy, because of slender
>    Aphrodite
>    (102)

Her power is also suggested allegorically by the fact that Eros and Persuasion are, according to Sappho, her children (90, 198, 200). Her influence, then, is felt in communal celebration and individual patronage alike, and in the momentary impulses of passion as well as glorious epiphanies. She herself is at once an allegory of passion, a majestic divinity, and an intimate friend.

Aphrodite was a figure who offered unusual opportunities to

the poet. Her significance goes well beyond the fact that she embodies sexuality: she is also one of the few positive archetypes in Greek culture of a female sexuality that is not confined to the functions of fertility and reproduction, and the only Olympian goddess to step out of the polar roles of active male and passive female. And she is treated in Sappho in a celebratory way, which contrasts with the overtones of danger present in many portrayals of her in Greek literature. To present Aphrodite as a paradigm and patron to a female audience, therefore, was to offer them an unusually empowering image of their own sexuality.

She is important too for the part she plays in the Adonia. Earlier we looked at the contrast between this and another festival held in classical Athens, the Thesmophoria. It is of course dangerous to argue from silence when so much of Sappho's poetry has been lost. But still it is striking that of these two it is the less strictly controlled one, the Adonia, that is represented in Sappho and not the Thesmophoria, even though the latter was celebrated in her time. In fact Sappho's poetry makes the earliest references we have in Greek culture to the Adonia, which is thought to have spread to Greece from the Near East. One of them is the snatch of sung dialogue between goddess and singers quoted in the last chapter, which is important here for two reasons. It indicates that the singers were young women, and it dramatizes their companionship with Aphrodite in mourning Adonis, who is her junior. This festival, then, by drawing its young participants into alignment with the goddess' desire, positions them too in a sexually active role.

The importance of Aphrodite and even the practice of the Adonia are no doubt largely determined by social factors, including the high value placed on aristocratic women's sexuality. But there are several lesser goddesses whose love interests follow the same pattern as Aphrodite's. Although we can make out little of what Sappho wrote about them, we do know that her poems mentioned two minor female deities who, like Aphrodite, sought mortal men as lovers. Selene, the moon goddess, came down to earth to meet her lover Endymion, while the goddess of dawn, Eos, fell in love with Tithonus and is shown on vase paintings either pursuing him or carrying him off in her arms (fig. 14). Also the semidivine figure of Helen, who abandoned her husband for love of Paris, is sympathetically presented in a poem to

be discussed in the next chapter. There is a striking contrast here with the poem in which Alcaeus contrasts the virtuous and passive bride, Thetis, with the disruptive and dangerous Helen.

Aphrodite's mourning for Adonis is echoed in the stories of two other mythical young men whom Sappho is said to have mentioned. Although no words survive, Sappho apparently sang of Linus (140b), who also died young and who is mourned in the dirge described on Achilles' shield in the *Iliad*. Then there is Phaon, often identified with Adonis and later linked in legend with Sappho. Again we have only a later commentator's word that he figured in her poetry (211a). But since Phaon is also a beautiful young man loved by Aphrodite, it is plausible that he too should have been the subject of songs like those for Adonis and Linus. And while the legends may have erred in attributing love for him to Sappho, they also contain an important truth. These beloved youths contribute to a celebration by Sappho of women as active lovers which, in the context of Greek literature as a whole, is astonishing, and which recurs in her poetry in more ways than one.

LOVER AND BELOVED

Much archaic love poetry was structured by the asymmetrical and hierarchical relations that were the norm for male lovers. In this structure the only position available to women is that of an object of desire. True, several of Sappho's divinities reverse the pattern, with a female pursuing a male of inferior (because mortal) status. But how does this work when both lovers are mortal, and female? Plutarch assumed that love between Spartan women reproduced the unequal structures of male paederasty, but I have already suggested that this may not have been so.

There is ample support for this argument in those poems of Sappho's that represent individual love relationships. Only one (poem 1) makes reference to the traditional lover-beloved, pursuer-pursued structure, and even there its significance is ambiguous. Elsewhere the most striking feature of her love poems is, precisely, the absence of a sharp distinction between subject and object of desire.

Sappho's love poems typically figure more than one desiring 129 female voice, sometimes but not always including the singer's, and there is a tendency for them to be constantly linked: it is as if the expression of desire is constantly passed from one voice to another. Several of the poems discussed in more detail in the next chapter illustrate this process, but it can be seen even in the following brief and tattered passage:

> . . . I bid you,
> [Ab]anthis, take [your ly]re and sing of Gongyla,
> while desire once again flits around you, the
> lovely one—for her dress made your heart flutter when you
> saw it, and I rejoice
> (22.9–14)

The speaker commands a second person, probably Abanthis, to take her lyre and celebrate in song her desire for a third, Gongyla. Clearly this is not the first time Abanthis has felt such desire, as indicated by the words "once again," which are traditional in love poetry and help to make explicit the poem's eroticism. Abanthis' attraction to Gongyla is then explained by a description of Gongyla as "lovely" and an account of how her appearance excited Abanthis. Finally, the speaker brings herself onto the scene with the words "I rejoice." Yet in a sense she has been implicated in Abanthis' passion from the beginning. She is in fact not a speaker but a singer: it is in song that she bids Abanthis to sing. Then she proceeds to carry out her own command, herself celebrating in song Gongyla's beauty. So there is an identification between the singer of the poem and Abanthis, which is only possible because of their equal status: both are singing, desiring subjects.

Fragment 96 shows that this process can embrace the object of love as well. Atthis' absent admirer was, the poem says, attracted partly by her singing: "she took delight in your song."

The singer of these words is performing through her own song an act designated within it as erotic, constituting herself as an object of desire. But when she goes on to praise the distant woman's beauty, she also becomes a desiring subject; and Atthis' admirer in turn is the object of the singer's desire as well as the lover of Atthis.

This constant movement of desire from one singer to another, blurring the boundaries between them so that each is both subject and object of song, praise, and love, cannot be imagined in the symposium. Debarred from the political power so strenuously figured in masculine love poetry, Sappho and her companions also escape the hierarchies and exclusions that such power imposes on the world. Male symposiasts sang to their peers, but not often about them; the youths and girls to whom their love poems are addressed were sometimes outside the sympotic group altogether, and some are obviously fictional. In Sappho's songs, on the contrary, audience, lover, and beloved all coincide, evading the polarity of subject and object that is so marked elsewhere.

Something of the same effect can be detected, though it is less developed, in Alcman's partheneia. The fragments of his work are even harder to interpret than Sappho's: the identity of the many female figures named in his choral songs is unknown, as is the singers' relationship to one another. But even in fragment 1, the longest and the most difficult to interpret, it is possible to make out that a group of girls, many of them named, are singing both to and about one another in erotic terms, and that here too there is more than one position available to each singer in the expression of desire. Here the chorus sing of another's desire in the lines:

> . . . and nor will you go to Aenesimbrota's and say
> 'If only Astaphis could be mine,
> if only Philylla were to look at me
> and Damareta and lovely Ianthemis'.
> (1.73–76)

The merging of several desiring female voices is one of Sappho's most characteristic effects, and more fully developed in her work than in Alcman's, at least as far as we can tell from these fragments. The fact that it is there at all in Alcman, however, shows how rooted her work is in the situation for which she composed. The guarantors of the circulation of desire through her songs are, as well as the goddess Aphrodite, the community of singers of whom she was only one.

To repeat the question from which I departed at the beginning of this chapter: how are we to describe Sappho's own sexuality? There is no question of reading sexual practices directly from Sappho's poetry or from any of the other discourses considered here. If I have laid heavy stress on public, collective forms of sexual expression, this is partly to counteract the modern assumption that sexuality belongs to the private sphere. I have also explored the reasons why the social identity of an aristocratic woman was an eroticized one, and how homosexual desire could be institutionalized in one of the groups for which Sappho probably composed: young girls en route to adult female status and marriage. All this means that we cannot simply call her lesbian in the modern sense without qualification.

But the likelihood that homosexuality was institutionalized at one stage of a girl's life does not close the question of how far it was a lived experience for Sappho. The similarities of expression between Alcman's songs for young girls and Sappho's poetry are striking, lending weight to the suggestion that she too composed for parthenoi, but the parallel does not cover all of her poetry. Alcman composed specifically for formal public performance by choruses of girls. In Sappho the range of performers, audiences, and situations appears much wider, including not only some poems addressed to women but also love songs in which the poet names herself. The perils of interpreting her oeuvre as autobiographical will now, I hope, be clear. But the existence of poems like the prayer for her brother's safety means that it would be perverse to argue that there is nothing of the poet herself in her love poetry, even if the voice may sometimes be mediated by poetic personae or may express loves other than her own.

Atthis' admirer in fragment 96 has left Lesbos, apparently without hope of return, and is probably now a married woman. But her companions, in a highly sexually segregated society, are still female, and it is difficult to imagine that the erotic tenderness for female companions learned as a girl has been erased by marriage. The case must surely be similar for Sappho and her companions. In Plato's *Symposium,* Aristophanes is credited with a brief allusion to lesbianism, in which he refers to women whose erotic preference throughout their lives, and not just in girlhood, is for their own sex. Encountering Sappho in her love songs, we can hardly doubt that she too was, as later antiquity declared, a lover of women.

In the end, however, the challenge of reading Sappho is not to separate the individual from the collective, or (especially) the sexual from the social and religious, but to reunite them in ways our culture has all but forgotten. We can perhaps best do this with the help of the female divinities who inspire her poems. When Athena, in book 1 of the *Iliad,* restrains Achilles' anger by tugging at his hair, she is at once a goddess of global power, a sign of the hero's favored status, and a sudden impulse in his heart. So it is with Sappho's goddesses. The presence of the Graces *is* the beauty of aristocratic maidens and the longing they arouse as they dance, as that of the Muses is their skill in making music. And there is a sense in which Aphrodite, that awe-inspiring figure with whom Sappho and her companions are on such intimate terms, tells us all we need to know about Sappho and her desire.

1. The earliest portrait of Sappho, in a drawing that improves slightly on the original vase painting

2. Sappho and Alcaeus

3. Phaon surrounded by admirers

4. Sappho reading a papyrus roll. Another female figure holds a lyre, and a garland is shown at the top.

ΣΑΓΦΟΥΣ ΤΗΣ ΛΕ-
σβίας ᾆσμα εἰς Αφροδίτην.

5. The text of Sappho's poem 1 from Estienne's
1554 edition of Anacreon

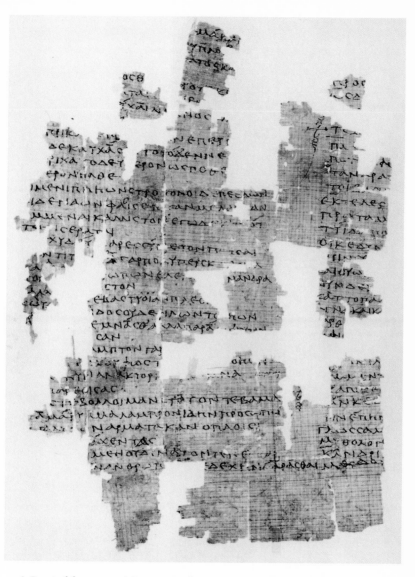

6. Part of fragment 16, preserved on papyrus. The poem begins a few
lines down; the right-hand column also shows part of another poem.

7. A bride, veiled and holding a garland, is taken to her husband's home. One of the women in the procession carries torches, indicating nighttime. Another woman, perhaps the groom's mother, waits to welcome the couple into the house. The shoulder of this same vase is shown in fig. 8.

8. Girls dance as two male musicians play the pipes and lyre; they are probably part of the wedding celebration pictured in fig. 7.

9. On two vases in a distinctive Eastern Greek
(Clazomenian) style, girls with garlands dance as female
musicians play the pipes.

10. A symposium: the reclining man plays the pipes
as a boy dances; a lyre hangs above them.

11. Two female figures
in a courting pose. The
chin-touching gesture
and the garlands have
erotic connotations.

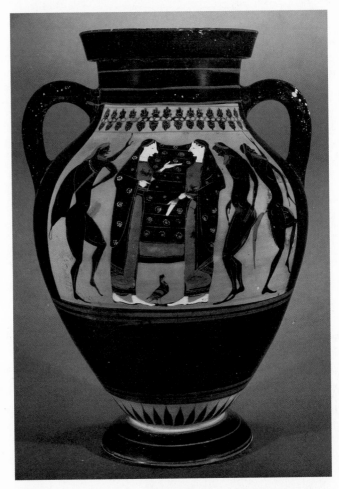

12. Two female figures share a cloak, in a scene with erotic associations. The satyrs show interest in them (the erect phallus of the wineskin-carrying satyr on the left has been painted out); the bird symbolizes courtship.

13. A man making advances to a youth, who holds a garland

14. Eos, the goddess of dawn, carries off Tithonus. The other side of
the cup shows his companions fleeing.

15. A procession of girls carrying flowers, on the stand of a vase from Anagyrus, near Athens

# 5. The Songs

IN THIS FINAL CHAPTER I want to give the last word to Sappho. The poems I discuss all bear the marks of the history traced earlier: they have been lost, found, selected, censored, quoted, misquoted, reconstituted, translated, appropriated; and the readings offered here must take their place in that history. What follows is one more dialogue with Sappho's daughters, her songs, conducted in the knowledge that there will be others.

This time I quote the poems in the verse translation of Josephine Balmer. Readers may want to compare them with the prose versions quoted in Chapter 2 in order to see what differences of interpretation can emerge even between versions that stay fairly close to the Greek. As before, I indicate gaps in the text; those who object to being reminded, yet again, of its mangled state will no doubt prefer to read the poems in Balmer's edition, whose unencumbered layout does more justice to their clarity and elegance. It also indicates the basic pattern of the stanza form named after Sappho, in which three matching lines of eleven syllables are followed by a fourth, shorter line of five. Of the poems discussed here, all but the two that deal with partings are in the Sapphic meter.

PRAYER TO HERA (FRAGMENT 17)

[Appear] to me, lady Hera, [I beg you]
reveal your g[raceful form]; for it was you who

[once answered] the prayers of the At[ridae,
illustr]ious kings:

after [many trials], both near T[roy and at sea,]
they came here, [to Lesbos] but they could not l[eave,
could not complete their journey home] until
they [had summoned] you

and Zeus, supp[liants' god], and [Dionysus]
Thyone's lo[vely son]; so [be gracious] now,
[send your help to me now] as you have [helped
others] in the pa[st]

*Holy and f[air]* . . .
*[p]arth[en]* . . .
*[a]round* . . .

(3 lines missing)

*[t]o be* . . .
. . . *[to] reach*


This much-reconstructed fragment is an example of a form extensively used in archaic lyric and in everyday life: the hymn, a
song to a deity. The versions that survive tend to be by successful,
named poets, and hence to be elaborate, but this poem illustrates
in a fairly simple form many of the essential features of hymns.
It is a call to the goddess to reveal herself to her worshippers in
an epiphany, and it begins with a formal invocation, honoring
her with the title "lady" and (probably) with a reference to her
beauty. Two other traditional ways of addressing deities in a way
calculated to call forth their powers are illustrated later in the
poem. Zeus is described as god of suppliants, a role particularly
relevant here; and Dionysus is identified by a reference to his
parentage. After the opening address, the poem reminds Hera of
a past occasion on which she granted help. Here, as often, this
reminder expands into a mythical story occupying the center of
the poem, an episode involving the two sons of Atreus, Agamemnon and Menelaus, on their way home from Troy. The text

degenerates into isolated words soon after this, but it is clear that the poet drew the usual moral, asking the goddess to grant favors now as she had in the past.

The deities and the myth in this poem both have local connec- tions. A similar hymn by Alcaeus (129) shows that there was a precinct on Lesbos sacred to this same trinity, Zeus, Dionysus, and (almost certainly) Hera; he too prays to the gods of his local cult, in his case for help against the treacherous Pittacus. The central myth in Sappho's poem is doubly relevant to Lesbos in that it concerns a visit to the island by an ancestor of the Penthilidai, formerly its ruling dynasty. The story of this visit is also told in Homer, but with subtle differences. According to Nestor in book 3 of the *Odyssey*, the two leaders, about to leave Troy after their victory, quarreled and departed separately. Only Menelaus visited Lesbos, catching up with Nestor as he pondered his route back to mainland Greece:

> We asked for a sign from heaven, and the sign came
> to cut across the open sea to Euboia,
> and lose no time in putting our ills behind us.
> (173–175, tr. Fitzgerald)

Sappho's version differs in two ways: it includes Agamemnon among those who visited Lesbos—appropriately enough, since Penthilus was Agamemnon's grandson—and it allots a prominent role to the Lesbian trinity of gods, who have to be appeased in some way before the journey can continue.

The difference between the two versions does not necessarily mean that Sappho deliberately altered the myth. The Homeric epics themselves simply represent one version of stories that were constantly circulating and constantly being reworked. As with stories of saints' lives in the Christian era, many different versions existed, often tailored to local circumstances, and Sappho's may simply have been the one current on Lesbos. But the very flexibility of the mythical repertoire meant that it could be manipulated in subtly nuanced ways. The possibility cannot be ruled out, then, that this version of Penthilid family history bore some relation to contemporary politics, even if we cannot reconstruct its significance.

The request, now lost, which was made at the end need not have been a personal one, despite the plea "appear to me" at its opening. As in Alcman's partheneia, groups of singers often used the singular I; or, as in some of the fragments quoted in Chapter 3, a soloist might sing in dialogue with a chorus. The damaged section at the end of the poem seems to include part of the word *parthenos,* which may indicate a group of young women as singers. If the poem's focus on the only goddess in this divine trinity is appropriate for female singers, it is even more so for groups of girls, who were often placed under the patronage of the goddess of marriage. But both the content and the form of this hymn as it survives are quite conventional, and it could have been sung by almost anyone.

PRAYER FOR A BROTHER (FRAGMENT 5)

> [Cypris and] Nereids, gr[a]nt that my bro[ther]
> will retur[n] here [to me] without har[m] and that
> [everything] which he wishes for in [his] heart
> will come to [pa]ss;
>
> [grant that he] atone for all his [fo]rmer crimes
> [and] become a joy to his [friend]s, [a torment]
> to his [e]nemies and let [n]o one [ever] cause
> us [grief again];
>
> [grant too] that he may wish [his sis]ter to have
> [her share] of honour, and wretched [sor]row
> . . . f[o]rmerly suffering
> . . .
>
> . . . hearin[g] millet-seed
> . . . acc[usa]tions of citizens
> . . . again
> . . .

*. . .*
*. . . and you, a[ug]ust Cyp[ris]*
*. . . set[ti]ng, evil*

This poem, the first of Sappho's to be unearthed at Oxyrhynchus
(in 1897), is also a hymn, but with a different tone and balance
of components. Now the opening invocation is the briefest possible, giving way immediately to a long and specific request.
Although she is not named, the number of references in other
sources to Sappho's brothers give good grounds for thinking that
this time she herself is the singer.

The surviving part of the opening line names the Nereids, sea
nymphs who had a cult center on Lesbos, as the deities to whom
the plea is addressed; the other name is lost, but it was probably
Aphrodite's. One of her other names, Cypris, or Cyprian, seems
to have appeared later in the poem, and like the Nereids she was
associated with the sea. Not only was she born from the sea,
stepping ashore on the island of Cyprus, but she was a patroness
of seafaring, often worshipped at ports (including Naucratis)
and other coastal sites. She and the Nereids can be thought of
as counterparts to Castor and Pollux in the poem addressed to
them by Alcaeus (34). Because of their links with the sea, all
these deities are obvious choices in a prayer for safety on a
voyage. They are also well matched with the singers making the
request: male singers address twin heroes, female ones a group
of mythical maidens and a goddess who represents love, as well
as being something close to Sappho's own patron deity.

Yet, apart from the choice of deities, and the probable inclu-
sion of the word "sister" (part of it is missing, and other reconstructions are possible), there is little to mark the perspective of
this poem as female. The sea voyage it implies has been plausibly
identified as that of Sappho's brother Charaxus, who was said
to have traveled to Naucratis to trade in wine. But the poem pays
far more attention to the errors he has evidently committed in
the past, which Sappho hopes he can now redeem. In her expression of this hope she associates herself, to an extent unique in

her surviving poems, with values and attitudes otherwise encountered only in the mouths of men.

The hope that by mending his ways Charaxus will become "a joy to his friends and a torment to his enemies" reflects a basic assumption of Greek morality. The world is divided into two camps, and it is taken for granted that an individual's prosperity will displease his foes just as it will gladden his friends. But it is also a matter of honor to treat each group appropriately, and several male poets assert with pride their observance of this code. The seventh-century poet Archilochus, for example, boasts of his aristocratic lineage and declares that he knows how to live up to it:

> You must have seen me as a low-class churl,
> not what I am and what my forebears were.
> I know the art of loving him that loves me,
> hating my hater and foulmouthing him
> (23, tr. West)

The poet Theognis expresses similar sentiments even more fiercely.

It is clearly aristocratic honor that is at stake in this poem of Sappho's, perhaps in the eyes of the citizens mentioned later. It is striking, though, that its most explicit expression relates not to Charaxus but to Sappho herself. In lines 9–10 she seems (here too the text is damaged) to have referred to the impact of Charaxus' actions on her own honor *(timā)*; and many translators have rendered this simply as an allusion to the relationship between them, a wish that he respect his sister. But the poem's concern with a wider social context makes it likely that her public standing has also been affected by his disgrace. These lines may well express the hope that in rehabilitating himself he will also restore the fortunes of his whole family, including his sister.

The poem does not say what Charaxus' misdemeanors were, but its talk of friends, enemies, honor, and crimes or mistakes indicates that they may arise from the complex maneuverings of

Lesbian politics. One effect of the constantly shifting alliances referred to by Alcaeus would be to confuse the distinction between friends and enemies, and so (as his poems make all too clear) to call forth vengeance on those who stepped over the dividing lines. Charaxus was probably caught up in the turmoil described by Alcaeus, and it is not impossible that his return is longed for because, like both Alcaeus and Sappho, he has suffered exile.

The more usual interpretation of this poem is derived from a story linking him with a prostitute at Naucratis. According to a number of later sources (test. 1, 15, 16; fr. 202), Charaxus fell in love with a slave-prostitute called Doricha or (in Herodotus) Rhodopis, and spent large sums of money buying her freedom; Sappho is then said to have berated one or the other of them in her poetry. The number of allusions to this story suggests that it had some basis, and the liaison with Doricha may have been criticized in another fragment, which also includes a similar phrase about former errors (15.5): some editors have taken the two fragments together, even though they were found on different papyri. The ancient sources that attribute hostility to Sappho link it with her brother's profligacy, and it is plausible that her main anxiety should have been for her family's name and fortune. But despite the expression of similar concern in this poem, there is nothing to tie it explicitly to the affair with Doricha.

Sappho's preoccupation in this poem with questions of honor raises some intriguing questions. Who, for example, made up this song's audience? It seems an unlikely poem for performance in front of members of an opposing political group: perhaps, then, we should imagine her sharing these hopes with an audience whose allegiances were the same as hers, so that like Alcaeus' political poems it would function as a kind of rallying call. Her concern for her brother is also striking in view of the fact that few other relations are mentioned in her poems, and there is not the slightest trace of the husband with whom tradition credits her. Elsewhere in Greek literature, concern for a brother is expressed by maidens, such as Nausicaa in the *Odyssey* or

Sophocles' Antigone, not by married women. It is tempting to think that Sappho wrote this poem when she was herself still a parthenos—but we can do no more than speculate.

### PRAYER FOR APHRODITE'S PRESENCE (FRAGMENT 2)

Leave Crete and come to me now, t[o that] holy temple,
whe[re the] loveliness of [your] apple grove
[waits for you] and [your] altars smoulder
with burning [franki]ncense;

there, far away beyond the apple branches, cold streams
murmur, roses shade every corner
and, when the leaves rustle, you are seized
by a strange drowsiness;

there, a meadow, a pasture for horses, blooms with all
the flowers of Spring, while the breezes blow
so gently . . .

. . .

there . . . Cyprian goddess, take and pour
gracefully like wine into golden cups
a nectar mingled with all the joy
of our festivities

Like the hymn to Hera, this song calls on a deity to make herself manifest. Here the goddess is Aphrodite who, though again identified by her link with Cyprus, is summoned to come to her worshippers from another of the places with which she was associated, Crete. This poem is yet another variation on the traditional pattern of the hymn. It is not clear from the corrupt text whether we have the beginning of the poem: it is very unusual to begin a prayer without even mentioning its addressee. But the symbolism of the central part soon makes her identity richly apparent: occupying the same position in the poem as the myth of the Atreidai in fragment 17, it too both celebrates and calls forth divine power. As in the hymn to Hera, the first-person voice in the opening line speaks for a group of worshippers.

*Sappho's Immortal Daughters*

For this "holy temple," unlike the precinct of Hera, there is no external evidence; no other author mentions such a place on Lesbos. But even if, as is likely, Aphrodite is being summoned to a place dedicated to her, no earthly sanctuary could possess the magical qualities evoked in this poem. Rich in appeal to the senses, Sappho's hymn summons up a mythic scene that is mysteriously empty of human figures: the altars smoking with incense, the water heard from a distance through apple trees, seem momentarily deserted. Yet it is filled with a host of symbolic resonances, and through them with the goddess' own presence.

On one level the grove is a kind of supernatural paradise. The natural world is caught in a moment that combines the perfection of all the seasons: spring flowers with roses and apples, cool shade with gentle breezes. Many other landscapes in Greek literature share this timeless perfection. In the *Odyssey*, the cave of the nymph Calypso is surrounded with vines bearing fruit and by soft meadows of violets and parsley (5.68–73); in a later book Odysseus comes upon the garden of Alcinous, where the fruit is magically self-renewing whatever the season (8.114–121).

But there are also many connotations of shared celebration in Aphrodite's grove, hinting at the presence of her festive worshippers even before it is declared at the end of the poem. In one of his fragments the fifth-century poet Pindar describes an idyllic afterworld, where the dead spend their time in a landscape similar to this one: "in bright-flowering meadows, / shadowy with incense-trees and heavy with golden fruits" (fr. 129). They also entertain themselves with games and poetry, and make perpetual sacrifice to the gods. This linking of sensuous surroundings, conviviality, and reverence is confirmed by Xenophanes' poem about the symposium. There too many of the features found in Aphrodite's grove and Pindar's afterworld recur: flowers, incense, cool refreshing water, altars, singing.

Most important of all, though, is Aphrodite's own presence. Almost every detail in the description of the grove is a reminder of her attributes, and hence of love both divine and human. Apples, roses, spring flowers, meadows, and horses are all linked with her in cult, and a poem by Anacreon brings several of these symbols together. The poet addresses a boy whose mother thinks she has him safe under her eye at home, and he expresses his desire for the boy by removing him, in imagination, to an erotically charged landscape:

> the fields of hyacinth,
> where the Cyprian tethered her horses
> freed from the yoke
>    (346)

And an early epic poem about Aphrodite represents her in clothes made by the Graces and the Seasons, dipped in all the flowers of spring:

> in crocus and hyacinth and flourishing violet, and
> the rose's lovely bloom, so sweet and delicious, and
> heavenly buds, the flowers of narcissus and lily. In
> such perfumed garments is Aphrodite clothed at all seasons.
>    (*Cypria* 6.3–7L)

These flowers, as we saw in the last chapter, are linked with love on many occasions, among them the episode of Zeus's and Hera's lovemaking in the *Iliad;* and the context of that scene is a pointer to the most powerful expression of Aphrodite's presence in this mythic grove. As part of Hera's campaign to distract her husband from the Trojan war, she seeks the help of two other gods: Aphrodite and Hypnus, a personification of sleep. With their aid she seduces Zeus, who then falls asleep; and Hypnus goes at once to tell Poseidon of this opportunity to intervene in the war "now that I have wrapped [Zeus] in a trance-like sleep" (14.359). At this point in the *Iliad* the powers of Aphrodite and Hypnus are represented separately, one making Hera desirable and the other causing Zeus to sleep. Their powers are united in another Homeric scene, though, when Athena in the *Odyssey* wants to excite the suitors' longing for Penelope. She first pours sleep over Penelope and then endows her with beauty by bathing her in Aphrodite's ambrosia. When Penelope wakes, she is aware of the enchantment that has been cast upon her, describing her sleep, just as Hypnus did that of Zeus, as a *kōma,* a state of trance (18.188–201).

It is this same word, *kōma,* that Sappho uses for the drowsiness that drifts over the grove, and its associations show that this too is no ordinary sleep: it is a trance induced by a divine power, whose effects embrace love as well as sleep. There could hardly be a more powerful way of expressing Aphrodite's presence in this holy place. As in the Homeric poems, her power is felt by mortals in the erotic spell pervading the grove, but it is not visualized until the last stanza. Then her influence is finally embodied: briefly she joins her celebrating worshippers, filling their cups not with wine but with nectar, and thus granting them their epiphany, a fleeting touch of the divine.

PARTING (FRAGMENT 94)

>   . . . frankly I wish that I were dead:
>   she was weeping as she took her leave from me
>
>   and many times she told [me] this:
>   'Oh what sadness we have s[uffe]red,
>   Sappho, for I'm leaving you against my will.'
>
>   So I gave this answer to her:
>   'Go, be happy but remember
>   me there, for you know how we have cherished you,
>
>   if not, then I would remind you
>   [of the joy we have known, of all]
>   the loveliness that we have shared together;
>
>   for m[any wreath]s of violets,
>   of ro[ses and] of [cro]cuses
>   . . . you wove around yourself by my side

and m[any] twis[ted gar]lands
[which you had] woven from the blooms
of flowers, you [placed] around [your s]lender neck

and . . . you [were] anointed with
a perfume, scented with blossom,
[although it was] fit for a [que]en

and o[n a] bed, soft and tender
. . .
you satisfied your desire *for . . .*

*and there was neither . . . nor any*
*shrine*
*from wh[ich w]e were absent*

*nor grove . . . [d]ancing*
*. . . sound*


With this poem we move into a more explicitly female world. Not only is Sappho named as one of the two speakers within the poem; the forms of the Greek words used for "weeping," "against my will," and "happy" make it clear that the other figure is also female. It is this poem and others like it, singing of sorrow over partings and absences, which suggest that the shared life of Sappho's companions lasted only a short time, coming to an end while many of them were still young.

As seen in Chapter 2, the incomplete text of this poem leaves two major uncertainties, the first of which is the identity of the speaker in the first line. This time it is certain, because of the meter, that we do not have the opening of the poem, which would have made it clear which of the two figures is speaking here. Many editors have given the line to the Sappho persona, but the calm tone she adopts later in the poem makes it more likely that these despairing words are uttered by the weeping girl. Grief-stricken at the prospect of leaving, she is comforted by Sappho with an apparently intimate reminder of what they have shared. Yet this poem, which seems confessional, shares more than may at first appear with the communal acts of worship represented by hymns.

The final section, damaged as it is, provides one indication of the links between this and the previous poem. Only a few words can be made out, but they are enough to show that the past shared by Sappho and her unnamed companion includes exactly the kind of worship illustrated in the summons to Aphrodite. Like the celebrants in that poem, they too have frequented sacred places—shrine and grove—and the last two words probably describe the form their worship took: choral dancing with, perhaps, some instrumental "sound."

Another feature common to the two poems is their symbolism. Like the description of the grove, the earlier part of the poet's speech of consolation includes details that evoke Aphrodite. The wreaths woven by her companion include Aphrodite's flowers: violets, crocuses, roses. She imitates Aphrodite too in adorning herself with them. A passage after the one quoted above from the *Cypria* describes the goddess and her attendants engaged in just this activity:

> Then laughter-loving Aphrodite and her handmaidens
> wove sweet-smelling crowns of the flowers of the earth
> and put them upon their heads
>   (*Cypria* 6.8–10L)

The use of perfume also links her with Aphrodite, who as she prepares to seduce Anchises is bathed by the Graces and anointed with fragrant oil (*Homeric Hymn to Aphrodite* 61–63). This evocation of past pleasures is, therefore, structured by a shared, almost formulaic symbolism, which also helps to locate the relationship in the wider sphere of shared worship. Sung before a group devoted to Aphrodite, the poem would soothe the grief each must feel on leaving it, but in a way that also asserted, celebrated, and sanctified their ties with each other and with the goddess.

The model of female beauty and accomplishment set out in

this poem also has its socializing aspect, tailored to an aristocratic audience. As she imitates Aphrodite, Sappho's companion is at the same time taking on not only the allure praised in Astymeloisa in Alcman's fragment 3 but also the role of the leisured wife as described by Semonides. The horse-woman, a fit companion only for rulers,

> is always washing herself—twice, sometimes
> three times a day—and putting on perfumed oil.
> And she always wears her hair combed out
> and shadowed deep with flowers.
> (Semonides 7.63–66)

So this song can also be seen as a way of instilling the appropriate virtues in its audience, no less than others in which the instruction is more explicit:

> bind together, Dicca, with your slender hands, shoots of dill,
> wreathe garlands around your lovely hair,
> for the Graces favour [a woman] crowned with blossom
> but turn away from those who go ungarlanded
> (81)

The formulaic aspects of the poem are, however, of only limited use in solving the puzzle of line 23 alluded to in Chapter 2 (whose is the desire, and for what?). The remaining letters of the line have set some commentators off on a quest to discover evidence here of physical lovemaking, although this approach, as I hope I have shown, risks being reductive in its approach to the poems' eroticism. The most frequently suggested reading produces a line translatable either as "you satisfied your desire for young girls" or as "you satisfied the desire of young girls": both, in this context, seem jarringly bald and suddenly impersonal. On the other hand, more than one of the mythical parallels cited above leads from adornment and perfume to lovemaking; and although physical love is rarely mentioned explicitly by male love poets, no one has ever doubted that it is part of what they are talking about. On the balance of probabilities discussed earlier, lovemaking probably was a part of the intense eroticism and sensuality surrounding the performance of Sappho's songs, but whether it was made explicit in this poem we cannot tell.

What this poem does reveal is that the socializing process of which it is part could be one of enabling besides (as many Greeks would have put it) one of taming. From one point of view a song like this can be seen as positioning its hearers as beautiful brides and wives, like Thetis in Alcaeus' poem or the aristocratic woman described by Semonides, helping to attune them to a role they had no part in choosing. Yet, even as it reinforces the cultural norms that fit them for this preordained role, the poem also provides them with ways of inhabiting that role which are far from passive. The symbolism it contains does have some directly erotic aspects. Sappho's companion adorns and perfumes herself in order to become attractive, as is shown not only by the parallel activities of Hera and Aphrodite but also in love poetry by men. The seventh-century poet Archilochus is among many for whom these same attributes are a focus of erotic description:

> She delighted in holding a spray of myrtle
> and the lovely flower of the rose;
> and her hair shaded her back and shoulders
>    (30, 31)

and

> . . . with perfume on hair
> and breast, to excite even an old man's desire
>    (48)

But the performance of Sappho's poem before an audience including young women would induce them not only to cultivate their own charms but also to appreciate the same in others. In celebrating female beauty in their companions as well as themselves, they are positioned as subjects as well as objects of desire, even the girl who is probably leaving to become a bride.

This would of course be true of any song performed by or for young women which celebrated their attractions, and there are some interesting parallels between this and one of Alcman's choruses. The singer in fragment 3 hopes that the object of her love, Astymeloisa, will take her own hand, which she describes as *hapalos*, soft or tender (3.80). This adjective is a conventional one often found in erotic descriptions, and in using it the singer also makes herself into an object of desire. The same word is used here in Sappho's poem, and to similar effect. As the girl adorns her neck with garlands, both the action itself and the poet's description of her neck as *hapalos* (16), translated here as slender, make her body a focus of desire. But not only are she and the audience drawn by the poem into the position of observers of her beauty—the same word, used later of the "bed, soft and tender" (*hapalos*, 21) on which she satisfied her desire refers to an experience of which she is the subject. In both poems, then, a female singer may be positioned as both subject and object of desire.

This kind of multiple perspective was, as we have seen, partly generated by the situation for which the poems were composed: for the female singers who performed them, eroticism did not entail establishing a dominant social identity as it did for men. Yet Sappho's songs seem to go even further than Alcman's in the way they extend and diversify the positions that female singers can occupy in the expression of desire. In this poem a move from the position of object to that of subject can be traced in yet another verbal repetition. The girl, lamenting the "sadness we have suffered," uses a verb, *paschein*, which can also mean, more neutrally, to experience. Seven lines later the poet uses the same word, but this time in a less negative sense: to translate literally, she responds to the girl's "we have experienced terrible things" with a similar phrase of her own, "we experienced good things" (11). The rest of the song echoes this change, transforming the girl's forced departure with reminders of a time when she was the subject of both action (she is the subject of four transitive verbs) and desire.

The multiplicity of positions in this poem is enhanced by another technique that Sappho also uses much more extensively than Alcman. It is because of an accident of transmission that we cannot say for sure who speaks the opening lines. But the first speaker's anonymity is easily accommodated within the poem's plurality of voices, reinforced by the fact that most of the poem consists of quotation. Generated by the girl's impending absence and the memories she will take with her, it looks both forward and back in time: the present moment sends out ripples into past and future. The poet quotes her own words of consolation, which reach even farther into the past; yet they are also projected into the future as a memory that will be drawn upon time and again. In this way her voice becomes a double of itself many times over, evading a single, fixed position just as her listeners could as they both admired female beauty in others and cultivated it in themselves. Perhaps this was her most enduring gift to her departing, weeping companion.

## PARTING FROM ATTHIS (FRAGMENT 96)

[Atthis,
although she is in] Sard[is]
her [th]oughts [of]ten stray here, [to us]

. . . [for you know that she honoured] you
as if you were a goddess *for all to see*
and, most of all, delighted in your song.

But now she surpasses all the women
of Lydia, like the moon,
rose-fingered, after the sun has set,

shining brighter than all the stars; its light
stretches out over the salt-
filled sea and the fields brimming with flowers:

the beautiful dew falls and the roses
and the delicate chervil
and many-flowered honey-clover bloom.

*The Songs*

But wandering here and there, she recalls
gentle Atthis with desire
and her tender heart is heavy with grief . . .

*to go there we . . . this not*
*mind . . . much*
*sings . . . midst*

*It is not [e]asy for us to rival goddesses*
*in lo[veliness] of shape*
*. . .*

(2 lines damaged)
*. . . Aphrodite*

*. . . poured nectar from a*
*golden . . .*
*. . . with hands, Persuasion*

*. . . the Geraestium*
*. . . dear friends*
*. . . no*

This second song of consolation echoes the first in a number of
ways. Fragment 94 takes as its starting point the moment of a
girl's departure; here we move on to a later stage. The former
companion of Atthis (who is addressed in several surviving fragments) is now far away among the women of Lydia, and each
grieves for the loss of the other. Like the previous song, this one
consoles partly with a reminder of past love: Atthis' friend in
some way (the text is damaged) treated or regarded her like a
goddess; even now, the singer asserts, she remembers her lost
companion with painful longing. But the poem also works a
transformation of this grief, setting it in the wider context of
shared symbolism and ritual.

The early part of the poem connects Atthis and her friend in
a series of corresponding movements. The beginning is lost, but
the first legible line shows us the absent woman turning her
thoughts toward her friends in Lesbos, a gesture mirrored by the

poem as it in turn describes her in Lydia. The movement of memory is similarly reciprocal: as the poet describes the woman's past love and present memories of Atthis, she is also offering Atthis a loving remembered image of her former companion. A third correspondence, however, shows the poem beginning to effect a sea change in Atthis' memory of her friend, in a way that also draws in the audience.

151

Just as her friend used to treat Atthis like a goddess, so the poem now presents her to Atthis in divine guise. The simile that brings about this metamorphosis starts from the woman's preeminence among her Lydian companions. Like many female figures elsewhere in myth and literature—Aphrodite, Artemis, and Persephone among goddesses, or Nausicaa among humans—she is pictured standing out from her companions. Her noble and conspicuous beauty is also expressed through a traditional image of celestial light, which is echoed both in Alcman (Astymeloisa is compared to a bright star in fragment 3.67) and elsewhere in Sappho. Two later commentators tell us of lines in which Sappho spoke of the moon outshining the stars, and one quotes a bit of the description:


The stars around the lovely moon
hide their brightness when it is full
and shines the clearest over all
the earth
   (34)


In this poem the moon's light is even more potent: it spreads over sea and land, and under its influence another flower-filled landscape comes into being, nourished by dew.

The power of the moon, implicit in this description, is explored in many other ways in Sappho's work. Among several fragments suggesting worship at night, one links the rising of the moon and a gathering of celebrants, shown to be female only by the pronoun used of them:

*The Songs*

When the full moon rose
[women] took their place
around the altar

(154)

The moon is also the goddess Selene, who is addressed in a
Homeric hymn and has a set of myths attached to her, including
the story of how she pursued a mortal man. In a lost poem
Sappho told of Selene's descent to earth to meet Endymion in a
cave (199). Selene belongs to that group of female deities who
take an active sexual role in relation to men, and to whom
Sappho's poetry seems to pay particular attention. She also
shares with at least two of them an association with celestial
light: not only Eos, the goddess of dawn, but also Aphrodite
herself have such associations, in Aphrodite's case primarily with
the sun.

Perhaps not surprisingly, then, the moon's influence in this
simile bears a resemblance to that of Aphrodite in other contexts. Her power to nurture plants is symbolized by her progeny:
according to Alcman (57), Dew is the daughter of Zeus and
Selene. As the moon's light spreads, the dew makes flowers
flourish, including the roses that are Sappho's hallmark as well
as Aphrodite's. This supernatural fertility is similar to that which
accompanies Hera's and Zeus's lovemaking in the *Iliad* or to the
grass that springs up under Aphrodite's feet as she first steps on
the shores of Cyprus (*Theogony* 194–195). Through these associations, the simile for Atthis' absent friend intimates that she
has the same kind of power to enchant as Aphrodite in fragment 2: momentarily, she is envisioned as a goddess, casting a
sudden, magical radiance. It is commonplace enough to compliment mortals by comparing them to deities. But here the comparison is taken to a new level by hints of an accompanying
power that is also superhuman.

Some commentators on this poem argue that it ends after the
seventh of its preserved stanzas, and that the remaining text
comes from another poem. But there are no external reasons for

thinking this, and taking the final scraps together with the rest gives us a poem similar in outline to fragment 96. Both poems, starting from the grief of parting, also transcend it, whether through shared memories or, as here, in a transfiguring simile that presents the absent woman in the aspect of a goddess celebrated by the poet and her audience. And both, it seems, contain this moment of grief within shared ritual.

The interpretation of the few legible words at the end must be even more tentative than usual. But it looks as if the allusion to divine paradigms is continued, only with a reminder of the distance between mortals and the gods: "it is not easy for us to rival goddesses." The next comprehensible phrase describes a divine visitation similar to that in the hymn to Aphrodite. Here too Aphrodite pours nectar, in a phrase that confirms the hints of her presence earlier in the poem: the same Greek word, *cheuein,* is used here as that which, in the simile, described the pouring of dew over the moonlit landscape. But now the action also marks the distance between the goddess and her worshippers, whose presence is suggested in the mention of a shrine (Geraestium) on the Greek mainland, as well as by the presence of (female) "dear friends." The relation between the two parts of the poem shows a delicate tact in the way it presents divine paradigms to its audience. Only in remembered absence is Atthis' friend associated with a goddess of such magical power, and then only through oblique associations. In the present, the second part of the poem seems to suggest, it is through worship alone that mortals can apprehend divine power and grace.

Within the dramatic situation of the poem, the consolation it offers seems less complete than that of fragment 94. While one of the two lovers is comforted with an idealizing image of her friend, the other's pain is unassuaged, and only the moon's radiance bridges the expanses of land and sea that separate them. But the poem's effects extend beyond this scenario. Not only does it evoke for its audience the figure of another goddess who combines beauty with active sexuality; it engages them too in the movement of an active desire that animates the whole poem. It is the very disparity between the two lovers' positions, juxtaposing unsatisfied longing with a quasi-divine image of female beauty, that generates the erotic dynamism of the poem, leading its female listeners to identify with the longing of the two lovers. And their desire is engaged in a way that, once again, aligns them with more than one position within the poem. I argued in the last chapter that the definition of Atthis' voice as erotic is symptomatic of the way in which the roles of singer, lover, and beloved merge in the movement of desire through the poem. Linked with this is another, even more important process of merging, which is achieved through the moon simile. As they share the love and admiration for Atthis' friend expressed through this image, the listeners simultaneously focus their longing on the divine power it manifests. In the image at the heart of this poem, then, individual love and collective worship are one and the same.

### THE LOVER SILENCED (FRAGMENT 31)

It seems to me that man is equal to the gods,
that is, whoever sits opposite you
and, drawing nearer, savours, as you speak,
the sweetness of your voice

and the thrill of your laugh, which have so stirred the heart
in my own breast, that whenever I catch
sight of you, even if for a moment,
then my voice deserts me

and [my] tongue is struck silent, a delicate fire
suddenly races underneath my skin,
my eyes see nothing, my ears whistle [like
the whirling of a top]

and sweat pours down me and a trembling creeps over
my whole body, I am greener than grass;
at such times, I seem *to myse[lf]* to be no more than
a step away from death;

but all can be endured since even a pauper

This is one of the two most famous of Sappho's poems, preserved because of the admiration felt for it by Longinus, author
in the first century CE of the influential treatise *On the Sublime*.
As well as quoting this text almost in full, he comments approv-
ingly on Sappho's treatment of love, the way in which she selects
and combines the most telling details of lovers' experiences.
Longinus' admiration has been shared by generations of subsequent readers, who have heard in this poem, above all others,
the quintessentially Sapphic voice of tormented passion.

It has also given rise to more disagreement than any other of
Sappho's lyrics. Controversy has focused especially on the scenario of the poem. The man referred to in the opening line has
been seen by some as a bridegroom, to whom the poem is an
elaborate compliment, sung at a wedding: this view was made
popular at the beginning of the century by those anxious to
protect Sappho from charges of lesbianism. Or, it is argued, he
is merely a figure of speech, a way of praising the female addressee by suggesting that to be in her presence is to be blessed,
or else that her charms are so powerful that only a god could
remain unmoved by them. These last two alternatives lead in
turn to differences in the interpretation of the speaker's symptoms, heightened by an ambiguity in the Greek: is she responding
to the girl's voice and laughter (as in this translation, "which
have so stirred") or to the whole situation ("which *has*")? The
speaker's sensations have, accordingly, been seen either as an
expression of the passion aroused in her (unlike the man) at the
sight of the girl or as registering her jealousy at the sight of the
two together.

Most of these questions cannot be resolved easily, and debate
will undoubtedly continue. We shall probably do best, though,
if we set this poem against the kind of situation and experience
encountered elsewhere in Sappho's work. As in fragment 22,
quoted in Chapter 4, one female singer responds to, and sings
of, the attractions of another, even using the word (*eptoaise*,
stirred) which in that song described Gongyla's effect on Abanthis. This poem too can be seen as a song in praise of the girl.

In more general terms, the situation can be compared to that of fragments 94 and 96. The singer's erotic admiration for the other female figure in the poem suggests that she is of marriageable age, and the opening scene contains several hints of a wedding situation. The man sits opposite the girl, assuming the intimacy of a relative, and he is compared to a god, as bridegrooms often were: these details have led recently to renewed arguments that the poem was performed at a wedding. Even if he is not literally a bridegroom, present when the song was sung, the scenario of man and girl in close proximity must certainly allude to their marriage, whether actual or forthcoming. For the female singer, though, it means separation, as described in fragments 94 and 96. Her passion can be understood as arising from the pain of separation as well as from the effects of the girl's charms, representing marriage from the viewpoint of one of her companions as an occasion involving both joy and loss.

It seems to be the singer's pain that has left the most lasting impression on many readers of this poem. One reason for this, perhaps, is the detailed way in which the singer describes the loss of her faculties: she appears almost to disintegrate bodily, and although the final, damaged line may suggest some kind of recovery, it cannot be interpreted with confidence. Another is the point at which the poem breaks off. The opening words of fragment 94 ("frankly I wish that I were dead") would have sounded very different if they had come at the end of the surviving passage, and it may well be that this poem too went on to transform the singer's emotions as fragments 94 and 96 do. Yet another factor is the famous imitation of this poem by Catullus. In his version, also based on the opening four stanzas, the speaker is a man and the woman his faithless mistress, and the Catullan adaptation has no doubt helped to color the interpretation of the Sapphic original.

Longinus' comments, on the other hand, show that he took the symptoms described here simply as well-known signs of "love's madness." But to judge from her other surviving poems, Sappho seems to have placed far less emphasis on the disturbing effects of passion than many male poets did. In the fragments of Anacreon quoted in Chapter 4, Eros was a violent adversary, a boxer or a blacksmith, and another image represents him as both powerful and unpredictable: "The dice of Love are madness and uproar" (398). In Sappho, love is by no means unmixed delight: fragments 94 and 96 show its pain as well as its pleasure, and elsewhere she calls Eros "giver of pain" (172) and "bittersweet" (130). But the violence of Anacreon's images is missing, and even this, her closest approximation, represents love's effect as far less brutal:

> Love shook my heart
> like the wind on the mountain
> rushing over the oak trees.
>   (47)

It seems likely, then, that it is grief as well as love that gives rise to the physical effects described in fragment 31.

The comparatively bleak impression created by this poem can also be linked with another unusual feature: the way in which the singer and her addressee become separated. In common with the two already discussed, this poem suggests an erotic relationship between two female speakers—the singer's voice expresses desire, that of the girl arouses it—which is in some way interrupted. But here the separation seems more radical, despite the fact that the girl is apparently present throughout the poem. The singer's concentration on her own sensations conveys a sense of increasing isolation, so that by the end of the fourth stanza, in the phrase "I seem to myself," she appears to speak to herself rather than to another. In fragments 94 and 96, although the lovers are either permanently separated or about to be, there is a continuing dialogue between them, bridging the gaps of space and time. Here the hints of an erotic dialogue between the poem's two female figures are erased after the opening lines.

We have already seen the way in which the expression of love passes from one singer to another in several of Sappho's poems, creating the effect of a proliferation of voices in which the distinction between subject and object of desire becomes blurred. Fragments 94 and 96 reveal more of the ways in which this effect is achieved. In both poems, distances of space and time between the lovers are crossed over and over again by the operations of love and memory. In the second, the multiplicity of voices is enhanced by quotation: as one lover's voice doubles another, so the singer's voice doubles itself, sending echoes from the past into the future.

Against this background, fragment 31 emerges as even more exceptional. There is no doubling of voices, the three figures occupy the same space, and the action takes place only in the present. Most important, the possibility of erotic dialogue between the two female figures disappears early in the poem, and this too can be read as giving rise to the devastating symptoms suffered by the singer: her voice falls silent, her faculties of perception desert her, and she disintegrates into a mere assemblage of sensations and attributes. The severing of contact between singer and addressee can of course be attributed to an external situation: the possibility that the girl will soon leave to be married. But it is paralleled within the poem by a division that is highly unusual for Sappho: a sharp distinction between the positions of subject and object.

Some aspects of the opening lines seem to suggest that the circulation of desire through the poem will involve all three figures. As in previous poems, the singer addresses a beloved girl, and in describing the girl's voice and laughter she implicitly identifies with the man who also takes pleasure in them. But this identification is arrested by a competing process, which can be charted through the repetition of a single word. The four complete stanzas of the poem are framed by the verb *phainesthai*, to seem, which both opens the poem ("He seems to me") and in the Greek text concludes the singer's description of herself ("I seem to myself"). It is used first to introduce the man, the object of her gaze, which for once is neither desiring nor reciprocal: there is no love, or even communication, in either direction. At the end of stanza 4 she also uses it of herself, and in such a way as to match linguistically the splitting that has occurred at the level of description. As Longinus points out in his commentary, she describes her bodily symptoms "as if they had left her and were external," and this tendency becomes especially marked toward the end of the description. Whereas the first symptoms are described from the inside out, as they are experienced, the expression "I am greener than grass" (perhaps connoting paleness or strong emotion: its meaning is not certain) represents the speaker from someone else's perspective, and the change is then confirmed when she repeats the word "seem." She now describes herself as the object of a gaze, whether (as the repetition of the verb hints) that of the man or her own, and in doing so she is forced to adopt a contradictory double perspective. As her body fragments, so does her own perspective within the poem, in a way that echoes the introduction, in that opening gaze, of a split between subject and object.

So it is not only the poem's content but also its technique that creates the effect of a particularly stark separation between lovers. Instead of multiple female voices, half-merging with one another as desire moves between them, this poem represents a different kind of subjectivity: one that draws a sharper distinction between self and other, and objectifies the other rather than engaging her or him in the circulation of desire. It seems hardly accidental that this mode, more characteristic of male love poets than of Sappho, should coincide with the presence of a male figure in the scenario, even if this does not by itself explain it.

There is no way of knowing how this moment of paralysis figured within the song as a whole, and whether it was contained within and assuaged by shared worship as in previous ones. But even without its context, the unusual features of the fragment do not set it entirely apart from others dealing with the wrenching separations that marriage must have caused. Whatever the occasions for which it was sung, all the singer's actions—complimenting the man, praising the girl, expressing grief at separation—can be linked with the situation of a girl's approaching marriage. Perhaps there was a particular reason why the balance of praise, love, loss, and consolation differs from that in other poems. But there are no private torments or solitary lovers here: though its listeners are not, this time, written into the poem as it survives, it nonetheless articulates experiences that will eventually be common to them all.

### SAPPHO AND APHRODITE (POEM 1)

Immortal Aphrodite, on your patterned throne,
daughter of Zeus, guile-weaver,
I beg you, goddess, don't subjugate my heart
with anguish, with grief

but come here to me now, if ever in the past
you have heard my distant pleas
and listened; leaving your father's golden house
you came to me then

with your chariot yoked; beautiful swift sparrows
brought you around the dark earth
with a whirl of wings, beating fast, from heaven
down through the mid-air

to reach me quickly; then you, my sacred goddess,
your immortal face smiling,
asked me what had gone wrong this time and this time
why I was begging

and what in my demented heart I wanted most:
'Who shall I persuade this time
to take you back, yet once again, to her love;
who wrongs you, Sappho?

For if she runs away, soon she shall run after,
if she shuns gifts, she shall give,
if she does not love [you], soon she shall, even
against her own will.'

So come to me now, free me from this aching pain,
fulfil everything that
my heart desires to [be] fulfil[led]: you, yes you,
will be my ally.

*Sappho's Immortal Daughters*

This prayer to Aphrodite is the only certainly complete poem of Sappho's we possess and, together with fragment 31, the most famous. One of the four songs to include an internal signature, it unites many of the features found elsewhere. Here the devotional and the personal come together in a dialogue with her patron goddess in which Sappho the poet represents herself as Sappho the lover, pursuing a reluctant figure who is now, despite the textual corruption, generally agreed to be female. It is one of the most engaging and immediately appealing of all her songs, and yet at the same time one of the most inscrutable. Aphrodite's words to Sappho, framed within a traditional format, suggest to many readers a teasing intimacy in the tone of their relationship, far removed from that of, say, fragment 2. And as in fragment 31, the pattern of this Sappho's relationship to her beloved is an unusual one.

The structure of the poem meticulously follows the classic pattern of the hymn. The speaker calls on the goddess with a series of epithets that both honor her and evoke the qualities on which the suppliant hopes to draw: her high status as daughter of the foremost Olympian god and her well-known skill in wiles and stratagems. (Her second epithet, translated here as "on your patterned throne," is variously interpreted: some commentators think it means "dappled in flowers," and some copies of Dionysius' text have a slightly different word meaning "many-minded.") A narrative at the center of the poem reminds her of a previous epiphany, and at the end the poet reiterates her plea.

Behind the narrative of Aphrodite's descent lies another model. The language of the poem includes some Homeric echoes, and the content too recalls scenes from the *Iliad,* especially book 5. The central figure of the book is the Greek hero Diomedes, who in a moment of mortal danger calls on Athena:

> Oh hear me, daughter of Zeus
> who bears the stormcloud, tireless one, Athena!
> If ever you stood near my father and helped him

in a hot fight, befriend me now as well
(5.115–117, tr. Fitzgerald)

Athena responds to this plea with a promise to help, only warn-
ing Diomedes that he must not fight any gods he may encounter
in battle. The sole exception is Aphrodite, whom he may wound
with impunity.

So Athena is shown as the powerful goddess of war, while
Aphrodite is singled out as weak and vulnerable, and the contrast is borne out in subsequent events. Aphrodite comes down
to the battlefield to help her son, the Trojan Aeneas, child of her
union with Anchises. But she is wounded and taunted by
Diomedes, and flees in her brother Ares' horse-drawn chariot to
Mount Olympus, where she is comforted in the lap of her
mother Dione. Zeus also advises her to steer clear of battle:

> Warfare is not for you, child. Lend yourself
> to sighs of longing and the marriage bed.
> Let Ares and Athena deal with war.
> (5.428–430)

Indeed, later in the book Athena is seen arming herself and then,
in company with Hera, mounting a chariot and going down
from Olympus to help the Greeks:

> Hera cracked her whip again. Her team
> went racing between starry heaven and earth.
> As much dim distance as a man perceives
> from a high lookout over winedark sea,
> these horses neighing in the upper air
> can take at a bound . . .
>                                    The goddesses
> gliding in a straight line like quivering doves
> approached the battle to defend the Argives.
> (5.768–772, 778–779)

In Aphrodite's journey to help Sappho, narrated at the center
of her poem, there are several echoes of these Homeric scenes:

the form of Diomedes' prayer, the yoking of the chariot, the journey from Zeus's palace through midair. But there are also significant differences. Aphrodite's chariot is drawn not by horses but by sparrows, which are associated with fecundity, and unlike even Hera and Athena, she does not seek Zeus's permission. But the most important transformation is in the role she adopts in making the journey at all: far from fleeing to Olympus in her chariot, she behaves more like the warring Athena when she descends as her favorite's ally or, literally, "fellow fighter." The opposition that Zeus drew in his rebuke to her, between love and war, is not simply reversed but invalidated: Aphrodite becomes the war goddess of love, and love itself is the battleground.

This transformation of Aphrodite may have a bearing on one of the most puzzling aspects of the poem: the nature of the relationship between the Sappho persona and the reluctant object of her love. The promises of Aphrodite allude to a pattern that, though common enough in visual and poetic representations of love involving men, is not otherwise found in Sappho's major surviving poems. Here we have the familiar asymmetrical model of male homosexuality: pursuit on one side and flight on the other, gifts proffered by an ardent lover and rejected by an indifferent beloved, and the lover's anguish arising not, this time, from absence or separation but from the coolness of the one pursued. The only case in which this kind of asymmetry is systematically represented in Sappho is that of the female deities mentioned earlier, and the young men they desire do not have the option of indifference.

Aphrodite's promise to Sappho has been interpreted in a number of ways. She may have promised that the tables would be turned and Sappho's beloved would eventually return her love. The two would thus, exceptionally, be able to exchange what for men were age-related roles, although this leads to the rather odd implication that Sappho would then be reluctant to respond. Or, since the text does not actually specify that it is Sappho who will be loved, perhaps Aphrodite simply assured Sappho that her beloved, now a girl, would come in her turn to know the pains of unrequited love when she, like a boy, outgrew the role of *erōmenos* and took on that of *erastēs*. Yet neither interpretation really explains why, here alone, the love of the Sappho persona should take a form so at odds with that found elsewhere in her poetry.

Perhaps, after all, the model for women's erotic relationships sometimes resembled that for men, even if no other surviving poem mentions it. Perhaps it is a matter of literary convention, playfully adopted here only in a poem that many have found full of teasing irony. But there is another way of understanding the pursuit-flight motif which can help to make sense of Aphrodite's warlike stance. It means assuming that the other figure in the poem is not in the same relation to the Sappho persona as the addressees of, say, fragments 94 and 96—or at least not yet.

In Chapter 3 we looked at some of the scattered lines suggesting that Sappho, like Alcaeus, was embroiled in the shifting political alliances of Lesbos. One of them seems to accuse Mica of having "chosen the friendship of the female Penthilidai" (71). In another, Atthis too has transferred her allegiance to one of the women identified in later tradition as a rival of Sappho's:

> Atthis, you have come to hate the thought of me;
> these days, you fly to Andromeda instead
> (131)

In these scraps the vocabularies of love, friendship, and alliance are united. The word used of Mica's (perhaps newfound) friendship for the Penthilidai, *philotēs*, is not only identical to that used for the love that Sappho, according to Aphrodite in this poem, hopes to win from her unresponsive friend; it is also a cognate of *philoi*, the word by which Archilochus designates the friends to whom he is so proudly loyal. It is possible then that the pursuit to which Aphrodite refers is generated by social and political necessity as well as personal feeling, and that what makes the girl desirable is her status as well as her person. In seeking her love *(philotēs)*, Sappho would at the same time be seeking friendship and alliance with the social group of which she was part; whereas Mica and Atthis, conversely, were deserting Sappho's.

This approach to the situation envisaged in Sappho's poem takes account of the way her world overlapped with that of Alcaeus: both were aristocrats, both suffered exile as a result of political upheavals, and so both were concerned with the shifting boundary that can so swiftly transform friends into enemies. It also helps to explain Aphrodite's warlike stance in this poem. Sappho's prayer to Aphrodite about her brother (5), asking for the goddess' help in protecting the family's public standing, uses a phrase almost identical to that in the last stanza of this poem ("grant . . . that everything which he wishes for in his heart / will come to pass"); and Aphrodite's part in Hera's distraction of Zeus from the battlefield reminds us that her erotic powers can be used instrumentally. If here too they serve wider ends, then she is playing for Sappho a role such as combat might have played for a man, and love is quite literally on a level with war.

Aphrodite's closeness to Sappho could also have a social dimension. In recounting this epiphany, which corresponds to those vouchsafed to Homeric heroes (and it is apparently not the first), the poet claims similarly favored status for herself. Other poems of which only scraps remain quote Aphrodite addressing Sappho (159) or conversing with her, again in the manner of a Homeric god, in dreams (134); and in a third someone, possibly Aphrodite, seems to have promised Sappho eternal renown (65). This poem can be linked, then, with others in which the poet boasts of her own future fame, and her account of Aphrodite's favors amounts to a public claim to the status by which the lover hopes to prevail.

Paying attention to the social dimension of this poem need not entail discounting the passion of which it tells. A poem that, to modern ears, speaks so clearly of the private anguish of rejected love is not now to be thought of as excluding such emotions: it is simply that they take on extra layers of meaning, issuing to the twentieth-century western reader the imperative of uniting what she is accustomed to keeping separate: personal feeling, social status, and political advantage. The poem speaks the language of love as well as of alliance: the renewed onset of passion is unambiguously signaled, as in many other love poems, by the repetition of "this time," and Aphrodite's power is described in traditional terms as that of "subduing." This kind of language evokes the other pattern common in Anacreon, in which love is an adversary who dominates the lover. But in this poem, unlike fragment 31, it is at least possible to imagine a social situation that could structure the singer's passion in the asymmetrical way represented by male poets. For once, Sappho too may have been just as concerned with the distinction between insiders and outsiders as any male symposiast. It is perhaps because this passion takes her over such a boundary that she departs, in this poem, from the fluid relationships more usual in her poetry.

This poem also differs from fragment 31 in the consolation it offers. Not only is Sappho the lover reassured with a vision of Aphrodite acceding to her requests; her passion is also both contained and universalized, in a way we now recognize as typically Sapphic. Whereas in fragment 94 the singer comforted the departing girl with a store of shared memories, this poem shows Sappho herself receiving the same kind of solace. The present moment is refracted into both past and future by quotation: quoting Aphrodite, Sappho reaches back through the goddess' words to a multiplicity of dialogues, in which the same painful desire evoked the same gracious response—and no doubt, on future occasions, will again.

### ANACTORIA AND HELEN (FRAGMENT 16)

[So]me an army on horseback, some an army on foot
and some say a fleet of ships i[s] the loveliest sight
o[n this] da[r]k earth; but I say it is whatever you desire;

and it is [per]fectly possible to make th[is] clear
to [a]ll; for Helen, the woman who by far surpassed
[all oth]ers in her beauty, l[eft] her husband—
t[he b]est [of all men]

[behind] and sailed [far away] to Troy; she did not spare
a [single] thought for her [ch]ild nor for her dear pa[r]ents
but [the goddess of love] led her astray
[to desire]

. . . *for* . . .
. . . *lightly* . . . w[hich
r]emin[ds] me now of Anactori[a]
[although far] away

[who]se [long-]desired footstep, whose radiant, sparkling face
I would rather see [before me] than the chariots
of Lydia or the armour of men
who [f]ight wars [on foot]

. . . *impossible to happen*
. . . *mankind* . . . *but to pray to [s]hare*

(9 lines missing)

*unexpecte[dly]*

This song, like poem 1, brings the categories of love and war
into a new relationship, but in a different way. Here the singer
begins, in quasi-abstract mode, with a meditation on value
whose terms are those of the masculine, military world. From
apparent acceptance, however, the poem moves swiftly to an
explicit challenge to these values, setting the individual
against the collective, love against war, and ultimately a single
female figure against the entire military might of the kingdom of
Lydia.

The state of the text poses several questions. The singer is not
named, but here there is not even a grammatical indication of
gender. And again there is no sure way of knowing where the
poem ended. Most editors think it ends after the fifth stanza,
partly because of the way in which it echoes the first, although
this argument could apply equally well to fragment 31, which
we know to be incomplete. I too make this assumption, mostly
because so little can be made of the remaining scraps; and I
assume that the singer is female chiefly on the basis of comparison with other poems.

*The Songs*

The challenge that opens this poem is framed in fairly conventional terms. Another fragment of Sappho's suggests that comparison with Lydia was a normal way of expressing high value. Speaking of Cleis, she says:

> for her, in her place, I would not accept
> the whole of Lydia, nor lovely
> (132)

The revaluation of ideals embodied in myth, implicit in the paradigm of stanzas 2 and 3, is also part of a long tradition in lyric poetry. We have seen Sappho drawing on the same body of inherited narrative material in fragment 17. Here the presentation of Menelaus as (if the reconstruction is correct) "the best of men" carries echoes of the kind of individual heroic prowess celebrated by Homer and nostalgically recalled by contemporaries like Alcaeus.

The critique offered through Sappho's mythical paradigm is distinctive in being offered from a specifically female point of view. Sappho places at the center of her narrative the figure of Helen, whose treatment here is quite different from what we have already seen in Alcaeus. In one poem, he addresses her as the woman whose "bad deeds" led to Troy's destruction and contrasts her with the virtuous and fertile Thetis (42). In another, her responsibility for her actions is represented as more limited: she was "crazed" by Paris when she went with him to Troy, leaving behind husband and child, and he is the one who transgresses the laws of reciprocal hospitality, as emphasized in the phrase "deceiver of his host." Yet that poem too goes on to catalogue the disasters that overtook Troy "for that woman's sake": the deaths of Paris' brothers and the doom of the chariots and the dark-eyed warriors (283).

Some of these details are repeated in Sappho's version: here too Helen's desertion of husband, child, and parents is mentioned, and here too she is linked with war. But the poem explicitly, defiantly, places an extravagantly high value on her love, and the only possible hint of blame, the verb translated here as "led astray," refers to someone else whose name has been lost, no doubt a divinity such as Persuasion or even Aphrodite. Helen is both blameless and the center of her own actions: Paris, in our (admittedly fragmentary) text, is not even mentioned.

The power and independence attributed to Helen can be linked to some extent with her immortal parentage. As the child of Zeus and Leda, she has an ambiguous semidivine status. In Sparta and elsewhere she was worshipped as a goddess, just as in Alcaeus' hymn (34) her twin brothers Castor and Pollux are prayed to for help. In the *Odyssey*, although the narrative treats her as a mortal, her exceptional status is indicated by a prophecy made to Menelaus: because of his marriage to Helen, the gods regard him as Zeus's son-in-law and promise him an afterlife in Elysium (4.561–569). She is shown in the *Iliad* in a close, even intimate, relationship to Aphrodite and has been regarded by some scholars as originally a double of Aphrodite; and her Trojan lover, Paris, is the least warlike and most effeminate of heroes. It is clear from all this that she has much in common with the archetypes already discussed: female divinities, including Aphrodite, whose power is expressed partly in the active role they take in relation to mortal men.

Sappho's celebration of Helen as an actively desiring figure accords with her choice elsewhere of divine exemplars of femininity. But what is also important is the way in which the poem positions its audience, and here Helen has a crucial role to play, anticipated by one of her earlier appearances in Greek literature. When we first meet her in the *Iliad*, she is engaged in weaving a tapestry showing events in the Trojan war:

> a double violet stuff, whereon inwoven
> were many passages of arms by Trojan
> horsemen and Akhaians mailed in bronze—
> trials braved for her sake at the wargod's hands.
> (3.126–128, tr. Fitzgerald)

Here Helen figures in her own narrative: she is both subject and author of the story, weaving herself into it just as she herself is, metaphorically, woven into the epic poem by its creator, the *rhapsōdos* (song stitcher).

Helen's dual status is echoed in Sappho's poem, where she is positioned in a chain connecting her with two other female figures: the singer and Anactoria. Again the link is formed partly by verbal repetition. The singer's question about "the loveliest *(kalliston)* thing" on earth is echoed in her description of Helen as one "who by far surpassed all others in her beauty," using a variant of the same word *(kallos)*. The effect of this repetition, together with Helen's position in the poem, is to hint that she is desired by the singer just as she herself desired Paris. And the oscillation between subject and object does not end there. Another verbal echo ties her to the absent Anactoria: the word translated here as "footstep," *bāma,* is formed from the same verb used to describe Helen's voyage to Troy, *ebā,* so that within the poem Helen's journey becomes a movement toward Anactoria. Thus the speaker is a desiring subject, and Anactoria, at the end, is a desired object. But Helen, in between, is both, and through her the audience is drawn into a chain of female desire in which each figure is both loved and loving.

In many ways, traditionally masculine values are more powerfully present in this poem than in any other of Sappho's. The armies dismissed in the opening stanza return at the end of the fifth as a measure of Anactoria's worth, framing the poem. This makes it all the more significant that, when Helen appears, gender categories themselves seem as fluid as does her pivotal role in the movement of desire. In sailing from the mainland to Troy and leaving her family, she imitates the action of the Greek heroes; but, at the same time, this assumption of a male role enacts a female singer's erotic impulse. In leaving her husband, the best of all men, to go to Troy, she both rejects and embraces the competing values in the first stanza—individual desire and military heroism—and the ambiguity is heightened by the fact that Paris is alluded to only in the phrase "to Troy."

It is in this disruption of gender categories that the challenge of the opening lines is most fully realized. Far from simply reversing established priorities, in what would amount to a simplistic call to "make love, not war," Helen's role destabilizes the opposition between them, and thereby unsettles the cultural definition of male and female. In the name of love, Helen journeys to Troy like a warrior, so that like Aphrodite in poem 1 she combines the spheres of love and war; placed as she is in the poem between female lovers, she also elides the roles of lover and beloved. Once again we encounter the Sapphic voice of multiple desire, reaching across time and space, now to undercut the whole cultural system of gender division.

One of my concerns in this book has been to situate Sappho's poetry in its cultural context, and to show how it arose out of her situation as an aristocratic woman composing for a largely female audience in archaic Lesbos. Social and political background alone does not, of course, account for every aspect of the poems: the range and variety found even in the pitifully small sample we have of her work is evidence enough of that. But some common patterns do emerge.

When read alongside other archaic love poetry, Sappho's erotic poems contain some surprises: in particular, the repeated appearance of female figures who take an active role in love and the fluidity of the subject positions available to the singers and audiences of her poems. Both features stand out in sharp relief against the work of such poets as Anacreon, whose songs treat women primarily as objects of desire.

Social context does play an important part. Aphrodite, the most powerful lover of them all, is an obvious choice (if indeed she was chosen rather than given) as patron of a group of women or girls cultivating the arts of eroticism. And I have traced the plurality of voices and positions in Sappho's poetry to women's partial exclusion from the world of the symposium, with its defensive stance against outsiders; this argument is supported by the similarities between Sappho's poems and the maiden songs of Alcman, in which something of the same fluidity can be found. Songs such as Sappho's fragment 5 and poem 1, which draw unusually sharp distinctions between self and other, may have done so because, like sympotic poems, they have an eye to the world outside the group for which most of her songs were composed.

And yet other features of the poems cannot be explained like this. What is it that drives the pervasive doubling and multiplying of voices in her poetry, and why does she show such interest in figures like Eos, Selene, and Helen? It is tempting sometimes to feel that hers is a kind of countercultural voice, speaking up for all those women who were veiled and led off to their husbands' homes when they had barely emerged from childhood. We do, after all, have the evidence of classical Athens to show that some men did sense in groups of women the capacity to break loose and threaten the social order. But democratic Athens was more suspicious of women than aristocratic Lesbos, and Sappho's high social status as a poet makes it unlikely that she was radically subversive.

Without other poetry by women from the period, and precious little even written for them, it will remain impossible to judge how distinctive Sappho's voice was in its own day. Some features may seem unusual only when set alongside the official, patriarchal line on Greek women, as if one were trying to form a picture of modern women's lives from, say, legal cases or advertisements. Even with more to go on, we would no doubt find that Sappho's relation to social and poetic conventions was a complex one. The poems dealing with the grief of separation might, for example, be construed as protests against women's lot, and it is worth noting that Alcman, who was certainly composing for girls' choruses, did not deal with it (as far as we know). Yet the shared expression of this grief can also be seen as a way of reconciling women to the partings that marriage made inevitable.

The last two poems, poem 1 and fragment 16, give us another glimpse of the subtleties of Sappho's relation to tradition. Both counterpoint love and war, and both play on the traditional association of women with love and men with war. But they also unsettle this association by confusing gender roles: Sappho echoes the prayer of a Homeric hero, Aphrodite becomes a war goddess, Helen goes off to Troy like a warrior. In the process all these female lovers place themselves at the center of the stage as mythical tradition has represented it.

In a sense, my discussion of Sappho's milieu parallels this move. Accounts of the ancient world have all too often relegated women to the margins of history, seeing them only as spectators or victims. My reading gives Sappho and her companions a role in archaic society that is no less central, and no less public, than the role of men: with marriage helping to shape social and political relations between aristocratic dynasties, love really is on a par with war. Although this system has been defined as the exchange of women by men, Sappho's poetry, with its celebration of active female sexuality, suggests that women did not experience themselves as mere pawns in the process. Clearly a more complicated model is needed which, without denying the realities of power relations, makes some allowance for the kind of active negotiation with social norms that we see in Sappho.

It is not only in the context of ancient history that Sappho's poetry has the power to challenge. How might we rewrite existing accounts of love poetry if her practice, rather than, say, Anacreon's, were taken as a norm? Perhaps most important of all, her forceful and diverse renderings of female desire still have a part to play in making it possible to think beyond rigid constructions of gender, and in giving voice to new possibilities.

I took the title of this book from the epigram in which Dioscorides hails Sappho's poems as her daughters. I would have liked to write the history of Sappho's daughters in a different sense, her literary inheritors in the ancient world: women who studied her, modeled their work on hers, and were inspired by her. But there was just not enough to go on. So perhaps her companions can be given the last word. The Sapphic voice is constantly singing to, desiring, echoing, and engaging another, its double;

and this characteristic mode is made possible only by the presence of a whole group of singing, desiring servants of the Muses. It was to them that Sappho uttered the prophecy that a chance quotation has preserved (147):

> I tell you:
> > in time to come,
> someone will remember us.

# Reading Notes

This section includes brief bibliographical details of works mentioned in the text and provides suggestions for further reading. Wherever possible I cite works available in English.

One in particular must be given pride of place. The Loeb Classical Library series (Greek and Latin texts with facing English translation) has recently published a much-needed new edition by David A. Campbell of the Greek lyric poets: *Greek Lyric,* 5 vols. (Cambridge, Mass., and London, 1982–1993). Volume 1, devoted to Sappho and Alcaeus, is invaluable for anyone studying Sappho. As well as all her fragments, it includes a collection of remarks about her ("testimonia") from antiquity to the Byzantine period. These are referred to in my text by the abbreviation "test." (e.g., test. 23). The fragments of Sappho and other lyric poets are numbered as in the Loeb volumes.

In quoting from Sappho and other ancient authors, I have in each instance used the translation most appropriate for my purposes, trying in general to quote poetry in verse translations except where a literal version is necessary to the argument. Quotations from texts in the Loeb Classical Library are indicated by the abbreviation L. Details of other translations quoted are given at the end of each chapter discussion below; where no translator is indicated, the version is my own.

Translations of Sappho in general are discussed at the end of these Reading Notes.

## Introduction

The question of Sappho's daughter is discussed in J. P. Hallett, "Beloved Cleis," *Quaderni urbinati di cultura classica* n.s. 10 (1982), 21–31.

On fictional biographies of Sappho and other ancient authors, see Mary R. Lefkowitz, "Critical Stereotypes and the Poetry of Sappho," in her *Heroines and Hysterics* (New York and London, 1981), and Lefkowitz, *Lives of the Greek Poets,* (Baltimore and London, 1981).

## 1. The Legend

Sappho's blank page appears in Monique Wittig and Sande Zveig, *Lesbian Peoples: Materials for a Dictionary* (London, 1980; French original, 1976).

Visual representations of Sappho are catalogued and described, with several illustrated, in G. M. A. Richter, *The Portraits of the Greeks,* vol. 1 (London, 1965).

Comedies entitled *Sappho* were written in fourth-century Athens by Diphilus, Antiphanes, Timocles, Ephippus, Ameipsias, and Amphis. Fragments of these are translated into a somewhat antiquated, and sometimes bowdlerized, English in J. M. Edmonds, *The Fragments of Attic Comedy,* 4 vols. (Leiden, 1957–1961). Also translated in Edmonds are speeches from two plays entitled *Phaon* by Plato (a playwright, not the philosopher) and Antiphanes, as well as scraps from several plays whose titles allude to Leucas. Plays by Menander, Diphilus, and Alexis, for example, are entitled *The Woman of Leucas,* Antiphanes wrote a *Man of Leucas,* and Amphis a *Leucas;* but too little survives of these plays to indicate their content. The fullest treatment of the Phaon myth is in Gregory Nagy, *Greek Mythology and Poetics* (Ithaca, 1990), ch. 9; the story is also discussed in a fascinating article by Eva Stehle, "Sappho's Gaze: Fantasies of a Goddess and Young Man," *differences* 2.1 (1990), 88–125.

Women are prominent in Aristophanes' *Lysistrata, Thesmophoriazusai* (Women at the Thesmophoria, also translated as The Poet and the Women), and *Ecclesiazusai* (Assemblywomen, also Women in Assembly), all three of which provide good examples of the stereotyped Athenian view of women as given to drink and sex.

On the Hellenistic women poets mentioned in this chapter, see J. M. Snyder, *The Woman and the Lyre* (Carbondale, 1989). Brief descriptions can also be found in *The Bloomsbury Guide to Women's Literature,* ed. Claire Buck (London, 1992), and essays on several of them are included in Francesco De Martino, ed., *Rose di Pieria* (Bari, 1991). All their surviving work is translated in Diane Rayor, *Sappho's Lyre: Archaic Lyric and Women Poets of Ancient Greece* (Berkeley and Oxford,

1991). On Nossis, see also M. B. Skinner, "Sapphic Nossis," *Arethusa* 22 (1989), 5–18, and "Nossis Thelyglossis," in S. B. Pomeroy, ed., *Women's History and Ancient History* (Chapel Hill, 1991); my account of Nossis is much indebted to Skinner's work.

The significance of sexual morality for the Roman elite is discussed in Catharine Edwards, *The Politics of Immorality in Ancient Rome* (Cambridge, Eng., 1993). On Roman attitudes to female homosexuality, see Bernadette Brooten, "Paul's Views on the Nature of Women and Female Homoeroticism," in C. W. Atkinson, C. H. Buchman, and M. Miles, eds., *Immaculate and Powerful: The Female in Sacred Image and Social Reality* (Boston, 1985), and J. P. Hallett, "Female Homoeroticism and the Denial of Roman Reality in Latin Literature," *Yale Journal of Criticism* 3/1 (1989), 209–227. A collection called *Roman Sexualities*, edited by J. P. Hallett, A. Richlin, and M. B. Skinner, is in preparation.

The two most substantial treatments of the *Heroides* are Howard Jacobson, *Ovid's Heroides* (Princeton, 1974), and Florence Verducci, *Ovid's Toyshop of the Heart* (Princeton, 1985). See also Amy Richlin, *The Garden of Priapus: Sexuality and Aggression in Roman Humor,* 2nd ed. (Oxford, 1992).

On the Greek cultural revival in the Roman Empire, see Graham Anderson, *The Second Sophistic: A Cultural Phenomenon in the Roman Empire* (London, 1993).

This chapter deals only with Greek and Roman antiquity, but a good deal is now being written on Sappho's reputation and influence in later periods. See especially Susan Gubar's classic "Sapphistries," *Signs* 10/1 (1984), 43–62; Joan De Jean, *Fictions of Sappho, 1546–1937* (Chicago, 1989), mainly but not exclusively on French literature; Sotera Fornaro, "Immagini di Saffo," in *Rose di Pieria*, 137–161, which takes up where De Jean leaves off; and E. Greene, ed., *Rereading Sappho* (University of California Press, forthcoming).

Ovid's *Heroides* is quoted in the translation of Daryl Hine (New Haven, 1991), which attempts to convey some of the wit and style of the original.


2. Papyrus into Print

The editorial marks illustrated in the mock damaged text of *Hamlet* are:

| | |
|---|---|
| .(dot below letter) | May be correct letter, but badly damaged |
| { } | Editor thinks material inside braces a scribe's mistake which should be deleted |
| [ ] | Editor thinks material inside brackets should be added |
| [. . . .] | Space for 4 (indicated by number of dots) letters |
| [[ ]] | Material written and then deleted by scribe |
| ] | Material before bracket missing and/or added by editor (used where beginning of line is damaged) |
| [ | Material after bracket missing and/or added by editor (used where end of line is damaged) |
| ‵ ′ | Contents added by scribe above line because not enough space |
| † | Text garbled at this point, can't be reconstructed |

The best general account of the transmission of classical texts is L. D. Reynolds and N. G. Wilson, *Scribes and Scholars: A Guide to the Transmission of Greek and Latin Literature*, 3rd ed. (Oxford, 1991).

The extent of literacy and the use of books in the century or so after Sappho's death has been much studied recently and is still a controversial subject. For general discussions, see Rosalind Thomas, *Literacy and Orality in Ancient Greece* (Cambridge, Eng., 1992), and B. M. W. Knox, "Books and Readers in the Greek World," in P. E. Easterling and Knox, eds., *The Cambridge History of Classical Literature*, vol. 1 (1985), 1–41. School scenes showing the use of wax tablets and book rolls are illustrated in F. A. Beck, *Album of Greek Education* (Sydney, 1975).

On Byzantine scholarship, see N. G. Wilson, *Scholars of Byzantium* (London, 1983). On the study of Greek in the Renaissance, see Rudolf Pfeiffer, *History of Classical Scholarship, 1300–1850* (Oxford, 1976), and N. G. Wilson, *From Byzantium to Italy: Greek Studies in the Italian Renaissance* (London, 1992). Muret's comments on Sappho are quoted and translated by Mary Morrison, in "Henri Estienne and Sappho," *Bibliothèque d'humanisme et renaissance* 24 (1962), 388–391; see also Julia Gaisser, *Catullus and His Renaissance Readers* (Oxford, 1993), 102ff.

*Notes to Chapter 2*

A brief and readable account of papyrus discovery is given by Leo Deuel in his *Testaments of Time: The Search for Lost Manuscripts and Records* (New York, 1965–66): ch. 8, "Pearls from Rubbish Heaps: Grenfell and Hunt," and ch. 9, "Oxyrhynchus Revisited." For a fuller account, also readable, of the papyrus excavations and the editing of the finds, see E. G. Turner, *Greek Papyri: An Introduction* (Oxford, 1968); discusses Sappho's fragment 16 on pp. 69–70. The recent discoveries in the Dakhleh peninsula in Egypt are described in *Mediterranean Archaeology* 1 (1988), 160–178.

179

Imitations of and allusions to Sappho mentioned in this chapter include those of Theocritus, *Idyll* 2, 106–110; Catullus in poems 51, 61, 62, and (probably) 68; Longus in *Daphnis and Chloe,* tr. B. P. Reardon, *Collected Ancient Greek Novels* (Berkeley, 1989).

Tony Harrison's verse play *The Trackers of Oxyrhynchus,* based on segments of a satyr play by Sophocles rediscovered on papyrus, was first performed at Delphi in 1988 and published in London in 1990.

On the texts discussed in this chapter, see Denys Page, *Sappho and Alcaeus: An Introduction to the Study of Ancient Lesbian Poetry* (Oxford, 1955); very technical, requires knowledge of Greek. More recently, textual problems receive attention in François Lasserre, *Sappho, une autre lecture* (Padua, 1989), which advocates extensive and sometimes startling reconstructions. For more accessible discussions of some textual problems considered in this chapter, see A. P. Burnett, *Three Archaic Poets: Archilochus, Alcaeus, Sappho* (London, 1983). The most recent scholarly edition of the Greek text is E.-M. Voigt, *Sappho et Alcaeus* (Amsterdam, 1971); previously the text of Edgar Lobel and Denys Page, *Poetarum Lesbiorum Fragmenta* (Oxford, 1955), was standard.

The currently accepted version of ode 1, line 24, is printed by Theodor Bergk in the second edition (1843) of his *Poetae Lyrici Graeci* (Leipzig). A long note in Latin in the fourth edition (1882) gives a full defense of this reading.

Ezra Pound's rendering of fragment 95 is discussed in Hugh Kenner, *The Pound Era* (New York and London, 1972), 54ff.


3. Poetry and Politics

An accessible account of early Greece dealing with aspects of its cultural history is Oswyn Murray, *Early Greece,* 2nd ed. (London, 1993), which includes a full reading list. See also A. M. Snodgrass, *Archaic Greece: The Age of Experiment* (London, 1980), which is more archaeologically based. Chapter 39a of the *Cambridge Ancient History* III.3, 2nd ed. (Cambridge, 1982), by J. M. Cook, deals more specifically with eastern Greece. The politics of Lesbos are discussed in detail in Denys Page, *Sappho and Alcaeus* (Oxford, 1955), though some of the detail is dated (e.g., the description of Lesbian society he excerpts from a nineteenth-century scholar, Symonds, on pp. 140–142 is best described as fanciful). A recent book that tackles the problems of writing a cultural history of early Greece, in a way inspired by New Historicism, is C. Dougherty and L. M. Kurke, eds., *Cultural Poetics in Archaic Greece: Cult, Performance, Politics* (Cambridge, Eng., 1993).

For brief notes on early women poets, see *The Bloomsbury Guide to Women's Literature* (London, 1992).

On poetic performance in early Greece, see the collection of excerpts, translated with commentary and introduction, in Andrew Barker, *Greek Musical Writings,* vol. 1: *The Musician and His Art* (Cambridge, Eng., 1984). For outlines of surviving archaic poetry, see G. W. Most, "Greek Lyric Poets," in T. J. Luce, ed., *Ancient Writers, Greece and Rome,* vol. 1 (New York, 1982), 75–98, and (in more detail) chs. 5–8 in the *Cambridge Ancient History.*

For introductory accounts of the symposium, see N. R. E. Fisher, "Greek Associations, Symposia and Clubs," in M. Grant and R. Kitzinger, eds., *Civilizations of the Ancient Mediterranean: Greece and Rome* (New York, 1988), 1167–97, and Murray, *Early Greece,* ch. 12. Further discussion of the social and political function of the symposium can be found in Oswyn Murray, "The Greek Symposium in History," in *Tria Corda: Studies in Honour of A. Momigliano* (Como, 1983), 257–272; Murray, "The Symposium as Social Organisation," in Robin Hägg, ed., *The Greek Renaissance of the 8th century BC* (Stockholm, 1983), 195–199; Murray, ed., *Sympotica* (Oxford, 1990). E. L. Bowie argues that much surviving archaic poetry was composed for symposia, in "Early Greek Elegy, Symposium and Public Festival," *Journal of Hellenic Studies* 106 (1986). On the social role of poets in this period, see Wolfgang Rösler, *Dichter und Gruppe* (Munich, 1980), on Alcaeus; T. J. Figueira and G. Nagy, eds., *Theognis of Megara: Poetry and the Polis* (Baltimore and London, 1985).

There is a rapidly growing literature on women in ancient Greece. For a brief introduction, see H. P. Foley, "Women in Greece," in Grant and Kitzinger, *Civilizations,* 1301–17. The revised introduction to A. Cameron and A. Kuhrt, eds., *Images of Women in Antiquity,* 2nd ed. (London, 1993), includes references to recent work. Two important new studies are E. Fantham et al., eds., *Women in the Classical World: Image and Text* (New York and Oxford, 1994), and Sue Blundell, *Women in Ancient Greece* (Cambridge, Mass., and London, 1995). On images of Athenian women on vases, see François Lissarrague, "Figures of Women," in Pauline Schmitt Pantel, ed., *A History of Women in the West*, vol. 1 (Cambridge, Mass., and London, 1992), 139–229.

On marriage in archaic Greece, see W. K. Lacey, *The Family in Classical Greece* (London, 1968), ch. 3. Two classic articles are M. I. Finley, "Marriage, Sale and Gift in the Homeric World," in *Economy and Society in Ancient Greece* (London, 1981), and J.-P. Vernant, "Marriage in Archaic Greece," in *Myth and Society in Ancient Greece* (Brighton, 1979).

The major recent work on girls' choruses, with particular reference to Alcman but also including discussion of Sappho, is in French: Claude Calame, *Les Choeurs de jeunes filles en Grèce archaïque*, 2 vols. (Rome, 1977); an English translation is to be published by Roman and Littlefield. See also S. H. Lonsdale, *Dance and Ritual Play in Greek Religion* (Baltimore and London, 1993), ch. 6.

An early and very influential contributor to the debate over Sappho's social context is Ulrich von Wilamowitz-Moellendorff, *Sappho und Simonides* (Berlin, 1913; repr. 1963, 1985). See also Reinhold Merkelbach, "Sappho und ihr Kreis," *Philologus* 101 (1957), 1–29; J. P. Hallett, "Sappho and Her Social Context: Sense and Sensuality," *Signs* 4 (1979), 447–464; E. S. Stigers [Stehle], "Romantic Sensibility, Poetic Sense: A Response to Hallett on Sappho," *Signs* 4 (1979), 465–471. A radically skeptical view of recent arguments is taken by H. N. Parker, "Sappho Schoolmistress," *Transactions of the American Philological Association* 123 (1993), 309—351; this, and the responses to it in the next volume by André Lardinois, "Subject and Circumstance in Sappho's Poetry," and Curtis Bennett, "Concerning 'Sappho Schoolmistress,'" both in *TAPA* 124 (1994), show how controversial the question still is.

The passages from Homer and Hesiod on musicmaking are quoted from Barker, *Greek Musical Writings*, vol. 1.


4. Sexuality and Ritual

The question of Sappho's lesbianism is discussed in André Lardinois, "Lesbian Sappho and Sappho of Lesbos," in *From Sappho to de Sade: Moments in the History of Sexuality,* ed. J. N. Bremmer (London and

New York, 1989; 2nd ed., 1991), which includes a full review of the ancient sources. The nineteenth-century controversy over her sexuality is discussed in Joan De Jean, *Fictions of Sappho* (Chicago, 1989), esp. ch. 3, "Sappho Revocata"; see also W. M. Calder III, "F. G. Welcker's Sapphobild and Its Reception in Wilamowitz," in Calder et al., eds., *Friedrich Gottlieb Welcker: Werk und Stimmung* (Stuttgart, 1986), 131–156. David M. Robinson takes up the defense of her chastity in *Sappho and Her Influence* (Boston, 1924). See also Edouard Fraenkel, *Horace* (Oxford, 1957), 346 n.40, for an account of a solemn recantation, in deathbed mode, by a scholar who feels he has wronged Sappho by accepting the "vulgar slander" about her. For discussions of fragment 99, see Lardinois, "Lesbian Sappho," n. 12.

182

For cross-cultural and historical studies of sexual categories, see P. Caplan, ed., *The Cultural Construction of Sexuality* (London and New York, 1987), and M. B. Dubermann, M. Vicinus, and G. Chauncey, eds., *Hidden from History: Reclaiming the Gay and Lesbian Past* (Harmondsworth, 1989), in which section 1 deals with the ancient world, and an extract from Judith Brown's *Immodest Acts: The Life of a Lesbian Nun in Renaissance Italy* (New York, 1986) is included in section 2. The poet Adrienne Rich's widely known discussion of the definition of lesbianism is "Compulsory Heterosexuality and Lesbian Existence," *Signs* 5/4 (1980); reprinted in *Powers of Desire: The Politics of Sexuality,* ed. Ann Snitow, Christine Stansell, and Sharon Thompson (New York, 1983). See also the essay by Martha Vicinus in Dennis Altman et al., eds., *Homosexuality, Which Homosexuality?* (Amsterdam, 1987).

For an introductory discussion of sexuality in ancient Greece, see Jeffrey Henderson, "Greek Attitudes toward Sex," in M. Grant and R. Kitzinger, eds., *Civilizations of the Ancient Mediterranean: Greece and Rome* (New York, 1988), 1249–63. On (mainly male) homosexuality, the classic study has for some time been that of K. J. Dover, *Greek Homosexuality* (London and Cambridge, Mass., 1978). Dover and others—e.g. Eva Keuls, *The Reign of the Phallus* (New York and London, 1985; rev. ed., 1993), and Peter Mason, *The City of Men: Ideology, Sexual Politics and the Social Formation* (Göttingen, 1984)—had already noted the links between the asymmetry of age and social status in erotic relations between men. But studies of social and sexual roles burgeoned after the publication of Michel Foucault's work in *The History of Sexuality,* esp. vol. 2, *The Use of Pleasure* (London, 1987; French original, 1984). Two influential collections of essays inspired by Foucault are David M. Halperin, *One Hundred Years of Homosexual-*

*ity and Other Essays on Greek Love* (New York and London, 1990), mainly on male homosexuality; and J. J. Winkler, *The Constraints of Desire* (New York and London, 1990), more general. Still more wide-ranging is D. M. Halperin, J. J. Winkler, F. I. Zeitlin, eds., *Before Sexuality: The Construction of Erotic Experience in the Ancient World* (Princeton, 1990). Artemidorus' dream interpretation is discussed in essays by Winkler (*Constraints of Desire*, ch. 1) and S. R. F. Price (*Before Sexuality*, ch. 11).

The different interpretations of Anacreon 358 are discussed in Bruno Gentili, *Poetry and Its Public in Ancient Greece* (Baltimore and London, 1985), 95–96.

On Greek views of female sexuality, see Anne Carson, "Putting Her in Her Place: Woman, Dirt and Desire," in *Before Sexuality*, ch. 5. Ancient discussions of the need to control women (Xenophon, Aristotle) are excerpted in M. R. Lefkowitz and M. B. Fant, eds., *Women's Life in Greece and Rome* (London, 1982).

The most comprehensive guide to all aspects of Greek religion is Walter Burkert, *Greek Religion* (Oxford, 1985). On festivals, see L. R. Farnell, *The Cults of the Greek States*, 5 vols. (Oxford, 1896–1909). On women's religious roles, see L. B. Zaidman, "Pandora's Daughters and Rituals in Grecian Cities," in Schmitt Pantel, ed., *History of Women in the West*, vol. 1, and the opening chapters of R. S. Kraemer, *Her Share of the Blessings* (Oxford, 1992). The chapter on gender in J. N. Brem-mer, *Greek Religion* (Oxford, 1994), includes further references. There are many discussions of the Thesmophoria: one of the most recent is H. S. Versnel, *Inconsistencies in Greek and Roman Religion*, vol. 2 (Leiden, 1993), 235–260. The contrast between the Thesmophoria and the Adonia, drawn by Marcel Detienne in *The Gardens of Adonis* (London, 1977), is further discussed by J. J. Winkler in ch. 7 of *Constraints of Desire*. Women were also prominent in the cult of Dionysus: see R. S. Kraemer, "Ecstasy and Possession: The Attraction of Women to the Cult of Dionysus," *Harvard Theological Review* 72 (1979), 55–80.

The Homeric hymn to Demeter is now available with a translation and commentary by H. P. Foley, together with a collection of interpretative essays, *The Homeric Hymn to Demeter* (Princeton, 1994).

On sex and the symposium, see the essay by J. N. Bremmer in *Sympotica* (above, under ch. 3). I discuss sexual roles in Anacreon's poetry in "Eros the Blacksmith," which is scheduled to appear in Lin Foxhall and John Salmon, eds., *When Men Were Men: Masculinity, Power and Identity in Classical Antiquity* (Routledge, forthcoming). On initiation and homosexuality, see J. N. Bremmer, "An Enigmatic Indo-European Rite: Paederasty," *Arethusa* 13 (1980), 279–298; Bernard Sergent, *Homosexuality in Greek Myth* (Boston, 1986); J. N. Bremmer, "Greek Pederasty and Modern Homosexuality," in *From Sappho to de Sade,* 1–14. On girls' initiation rites, in addition to Calame, *Les Choeurs de jeunes filles,* see Christiane Sourvinou-Inwood, *Studies in Girls' Transitions* (Athens, 1988), and Ken Dowden, *Death and the Maiden: Girls' Initiation Rites in Greek Mythology* (London, 1989). See also Wolfgang Rösler, "Homoerotik und Initiation, über Sappho," in T. Stemmler, ed., *Homoerotische Lyrik* (Tübingen, 1992), 43–54.

The range of archaic and classical vase paintings generally agreed to show female homoeroticism has until recently been tiny: e.g., Dover, *Greek Homosexuality,* 173, and Keuls, *Reign of the Phallus,* 85–86. But this picture seems set to be revolutionized by, among others, Gundel Koch-Harnach, *Erotische Symbole* (Berlin, 1989), who finds eroticism between women represented by such things as the sharing of cloaks and the use of symbols such as lotus flowers. A study by Keith DeVries of visual representations of homoeroticism, *Homosexuality and the Athenian Democracy,* is in preparation.

The prominence of active female divinities in Sappho and the subject positions of lover and beloved in her poetry are discussed in Eva Stehle, "Sappho's Gaze," *differences* 2.1 (1990). See also my "Sappho and the Other Woman," in S. Mills, ed., *Language and Gender* (London, 1995).

Sappho's fragment 22 has recently been discussed in J. M. Snyder, "The Configuration of Desire in Sappho," *Helios* 21/1 (Spring 1994), 3–8, which elucidates some of the textual problems.

Homer's *Iliad* is quoted in the translation by Robert Fitzgerald (New York, 1974).

## 5. The Songs

The list of recent publications on Sappho is enormous, and I mention here only a select few. Most articles in classical journals contain untranslated Greek, but I have included some in which the Greek may not unduly hinder understanding of the argument. Books that have particularly influenced my discussion and deal with the poems in more detail are A. P. Burnett, *Three Archaic Poets: Archilochus, Alcaeus, Sappho* (London, 1983), and Leah Rissmann, *Love as War: Homeric Allusion in the Poetry of Sappho* (Königstein, 1983). The extent of the Homeric poems' direct influence on Sappho has been disputed, however, as in R. L. Fowler, *The Nature of Early Greek Lyric: Three Preliminary Studies* (Buffalo and London, 1987). See also G. M. Kirkwood, *Early Greek Monody: The History of a Poetic Type* (Ithaca, 1974), though many would now dispute this sharp distinction between solo and choral lyric, and Bruno Gentili, *Poetry and Its Public in Ancient Greece* (Baltimore and London, 1985), esp. ch. 6, "The Ways of Love in *Thiasos* and Symposium," which is stimulating if sometimes idiosyncratic.

Important articles on Sappho's poetry, in addition to those already mentioned, include Giuliana Lanata, "Sul linguaggio amoroso di Saffo," *Quaderni urbinati di cultura classica* 2 (1966), 63–79; C. P. Segal, "Eros and Incantation: Sappho and Oral Poetry," *Arethusa* 7 (1974), 138–160; J. D. Marry, "Sappho and the Heroic Ideal, *erōtos aretē*," *Arethusa* 12 (1979), 71–92; Eva Stigers [Stehle], "Sappho's Private World," in H. P. Foley, ed., *Reflections of Women in Antiquity* (New York and London, 1981), 45–61; J. J. Winkler, "Gardens of the Nymphs: Public and Private in Sappho's Lyrics," in Foley, ed.; Jesper Svenbro, "La Stratégie d'amour. Modèle de guerre et théorie d'amour dans la poésie de Sappho," *Quaderni di storia* 19 (1984) 57–79; M. B. Skinner, "Woman and Language in Archaic Greece, or, Why Is Sappho a Woman?" in N. S. Rabinowitz and A. Richlin, eds., *Feminist Theory and the Classics* (New York and London, 1993); M. B. Skinner, "Aphrodite Garlanded: Eros and Poetic Creativity in Sappho and Nossis," in De Martino, ed., *Rose di Pieria* (Bari, 1991), 77–96. See also the collection edited by E. Greene (University of California Press, forthcoming).

Publications about Sappho by scholars between 1952 and 1985 are surveyed by D. E. Gerber in the journal *Classical World*: "A Survey of Publications on Greek Lyric Poetry since 1952," 61 (1968), 317–322; "Studies in Greek Lyric Poetry, 1967–1975," 70 (1976), 106–115; "Studies in Greek Lyric Poetry, 1975–1985," 81 (1987–88), 132–144. For a summary of studies and texts of Sappho from the seventeenth century on, see Helmut Saake, *Sapphostudien* (Paderborn, 1971), 13–36.

*Fragment 2:* Thomas McEvilley, "Sappho, Fragment 2," *Phoenix* 26 (1972), 323–333; J. M. Bremer, "The Meadow of Love and Two Passages in Euripides' *Hippolytus*," *Mnemosyne* 28 (1975), 268–280.

*Fragment 94:* Thomas McEvilley, "Sappho, Fragment 94," *Phoenix* 25 (1971), 1–11; A. P. Burnett, "Desire and Memory," *Classical Philology*

74 (1979), 16–27; Emmet Robbins, "Who's Dying in Sappho, Fr. 94?", *Phoenix* 44 (1990), 111–121.

*Fragment 96:* Thomas McEvilley, "Sapphic Imagery and Fr. 96," *Hermes* 101 (1973) 257–278; Rebecca Hague, "Sappho's Consolation for Atthis," *American Journal of Philology* 105 (1984), 29–36.

*Fragment 31:* G. L. Koniaris, "On Sappho, Fr. 31 (L-P)," *Philologus* 112 (1968), 173–186; Thomas McEvilley, "Sappho, fragment 31: The Face behind the Mask," *Phoenix* 32 (1978), 1–18; Joachim Latacz, "Realität und Imagination. Eine neue Lyrik-Theorie und Sappho's *phainetai moi kēnos*-Lied," *Museum Helveticum* 42 (1985), 67–94; Anne Carson, *Eros the Bittersweet* (Princeton, 1986), 12–17. On the meaning of the word *chlōros* (green) in this poem, see Eleanor Irwin, *Colour Terms in Greek Poetry* (Toronto, 1974), 65–67.

On Sappho's poem and the imitation by Catullus, see Dolores O'Higgins, "Sappho's Splintered Tongue: Silence in Sappho 31 and Catullus 51," *American Journal of Philology* 111 (1990), 156–167.

*Poem 1:* M. C. J. Putnam, "*Throna* and Sappho 1.1," *Classical Journal* 56 (1961), 79–83; Anne Giacomelli [Carson], "The Justice of Aphrodite in Sappho, Fr. 1," *Transactions of the American Philological Association* 110 (1980), 135–142.

*Fragment 16:* Page duBois, "Sappho and Helen," *Arethusa* 11 (1978), 88–99; Claude Calame, "Sappho et Hélène. Le mythe comme argumentation narrative," in J. Delorme, ed., *Parole, figure, parole* (Lyon, 1987) 209–229; W. H. Race, "Sappho, Fr. 16 L-P, and Alkaios, Fr. 42 L-P: Romantic and Classical Strains in Lesbian Lyric," *Classical Journal* 85 (1989), 16–33.

Archilochus 23 is quoted in the translation of M. L. West, *Greek Lyric Poetry* (Oxford, 1994), and the *Iliad* extracts in Robert Fitzgerald's version (New York, 1974). Translations of Sappho are from Josephine Balmer, *Sappho: Poems and Fragments,* 2nd ed. (Newcastle, 1992).

## Translations of Sappho

Many translators have responded to the challenge posed by Sappho's deceptively simple poems. No English version could reproduce their exact literal meaning together with their impact as poetry. Reproducing their sound, though it has been tried, is even more difficult. Ancient Greek poetry did not use the rhythmical stress patterns of modern English verse: instead it was based on sequences of long and short syllables which could be quite intricate (though Sappho's are not especially so); and it did not rhyme. So modern translators are forced to choose between sometimes conflicting priorities.

At one extreme are literal prose versions such as David Campbell's in the Loeb edition, which is based on an up-to-date text and shows clearly what is missing or conjectural in it. At the other end are those in which Sappho's songs are recreated in English verse, a truer translation in one sense but far less literal. Among the latter are Mary Barnard, *Sappho: A New Translation* (Berkeley, 1958), and Willis Barnstone, *Sappho* (New York, 1963), and his *Greek Lyric Poetry,* (New York, 1988). Both are well worth reading for a sense of Sappho's work as poetry, but both rely on now outdated texts and incorporate a good deal of interpretation and reconstruction: as in Barnard's opening-line-cum-titles (explained in her note on 105–106); and in Barnstone's titles, also his addition, and poems such as his number 142, most of which was concocted by a famously overzealous editor in the 1920s.

Most versions fall somewhere between these two extremes. Of verse translations based on a modern text which include most of the fragments, the most successful in combining accuracy with some of Sappho's grace and clarity are Josephine Balmer's *Sappho* (1992) and Diane Rayor's *Sappho's Lyre* (1991). Both also reflect the fragmentary state of the originals; Rayor's layout and critical markings are particularly helpful in this regard. Guy Davenport, *Archilochos, Sappho, Alkman* (Berkeley and London, 1980), sometimes stays close to the text but sometimes, unpredictably, takes off to create images that are only the translator's. The versions in M. L. West's *Greek Lyric Poetry* (Oxford, 1994) have the merit of being by a philologist who has worked on the original text (and sometimes translates his preferred reconstructions); but as English verse they are uneven, mixing linguistic registers to odd effect. Barbara H. Fowler, *Archaic Greek Poetry* (Madison, Wisconsin, and London, 1992), also stays quite close to the text, indicating some gaps but not all.

The major fragments are included in Peter Bing and Rip Cohen, *Games of Venus* (New York and London, 1991), which usefully attempts to match the original in such devices as the distribution of words between lines and repeated words. Richard Lattimore, *Greek Lyrics,* 2nd ed. (Chicago, 1960), produces wordier-than-usual versions with no attempt to represent the gaps.

# Illustration Credits

1 The earliest portrait of Sappho. Attic hydria (water jar), late sixth century BCE. Warsaw 142333. Czartoryski Collection, National Museum, Warsaw. Drawing from G. Perrot and C. Chipiez, *Histoire de l'art dans l'antiquité* (Paris, 1914), vol. 10, p. 241.

2 Sappho and Alcaeus. Attic black-figure kalathos-psykter (wine cooler), first half of fifth century BCE. Munich 2416. Reproduced by permission of the Staatliche Antikensammlungen und Glyptothek, Munich.

3 Phaon and admirers. Attic red-figure calyx-krater (mixing bowl for wine), late fifth century BCE. Palermo 2187. Reproduced by permission of the Archaeological Museum, Palermo.

4 Sappho reading. Attic red-figure hydria (water jar), mid to late fifth century BCE. Athens NM 1260. Reproduced by permission of the National Museum, Athens.

5 A text of poem 1. Henri Estienne, *Anacreontis Teij odae. Ab Henrico Stephano luce et latinitate nunc primum donatae* (Paris, 1554). Reproduced by permission of the British Library, London; BL pressmark 671.b.13.

6 Part of fragment 16. Oxyrhynchus papyrus 1231, second century CE. Bodleian Library, Oxford, MS Gr. Class. c. 76/1 (P). Reproduced by permission of the Bodleian Library, Oxford, and of the Committee of the Egypt Exploration Society.

7,8 A wedding celebration. Attic black-figure lekythos (oil jar), mid to late sixth century BCE. Reproduced by permission of the Metropolitan Museum of Art, New York. Purchase, Walter C. Baker Gift, 1956 (56.11.1). Rollout photograph by Justin Kerr.

9 Girls making music. Amphoras (storage jars) from Egypt (left) and

from Clazomenae (right), mid sixth century BCE. Berlin 4530 and 4531.

10    A symposium. Interior of Attic red-figure cup, early fifth century BCE. Lewis Collection, Corpus Christi College, Cambridge, no. 50. Reproduced by permission of the Master and Fellows of Corpus Christi College and of the Fitzwilliam Museum, Cambridge. Copyright Fitzwilliam Museum.

11    Two female figures. Plate in the Thera Museum, Santorini, late seventh century BCE. Reproduced by permission of the Greek Archaeological Service (Cycladic Ephorate). Photograph, Maurice Howard.

12    Sharing a cloak. Attic black-figure amphora (storage jar), sixth century BCE. London B163. Copyright British Museum.

13    A man making advances. Attic black-figure neck-amphora (storage jar), second half of sixth century BCE. Munich 1468. Reproduced by permission of the Staatliche Antikensammlungen und Glyptothek, Munich.

14    Eos and Tithonus. Attic red-figure skyphos (mug-like cup), first half of fifth century BCE. Lewis Collection, Corpus Christi College, no. 57. Reproduced by permission of the Master and Fellows of Corpus Christi College and of the Fitzwilliam Museum, Cambridge. Copyright Fitzwilliam Museum.

15    A procession of girls. Attic black-figure skyphos-krater (cup or bowl), late seventh century BCE. Athens, NM 16384. Reproduced by permission of the National Museum, Athens.

*Illustration Credits*

# Index